The Fighter & 'The Few'

SPITFIRE

— FLYING LEGEND —

JOHN DIBBS AND TONY HOLMES

FOREWORD BY AIR COMMODORE ALAN DEERE
DSO, CBE, DFC AND BAR

THE FIGHTER & 'THE FEW'

For my Mother and Father and for the late John Holmes who, as one of the unsung 'Few', kept No 74 Sqn's Spitfires flying during the long, desperate, summer of 1940

First published in Great Britain in 1996
by Osprey Publishing, Midland House, West Way, Botley, Oxford OX2 0PH

This edition published 1999
Sixth impression 2007

ISBN 978 1 84135 012 7

Written and edited by Tony Holmes
Art direction by Mike Moule
Designed by Tony Truscott of TT Designs

Printed in China

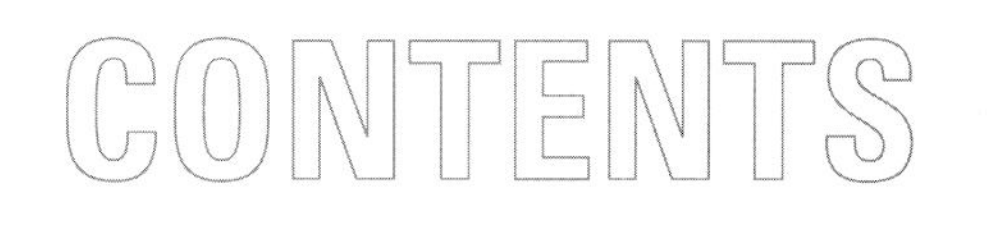

FOREWORD

'I fell in love with her the moment I was introduced. I was captivated by her sheer beauty; she was slimly built with a beautifully proportioned body and graceful curves just where they should be.'

Thus spoke Lord Balfour, the then Under-Secretary of State for Air, when, in the Summer of 1938, he was first introduced to the Spitfire. This appraisal by one who had distinguished himself as a pilot in World War 1 set the seal of fame of an aircraft which was to become a legend in World War 2. Increasingly as the war years rolled on, the Spitfire was to prove that her 'beautifully proportioned body' hid the frame of a tough little fighter which, in the skilful hands of RAF fighter pilots, was to prove supreme in aerial combat throughout World War 2.

It was in the Spring of 1939 when I made my acquaintance with the Spitfire. It was at Supermarine's site at Eastleigh airfield, where I had gone to collect No 54 Sqn's first Spitfire, a replacement for our now outdated Gladiator biplane fighter.

Even over this distance of time I can recall the thrill of that momentous occasion. As I sat in the cockpit ready to take-off I was beset by the feeling of completeness which was never to leave me in the years ahead, despite the necessitudes of combat. Indeed, in a dogfight I always felt that my Spitfire and I were as one – we certainly grew up together.

The photographs accompanying the text in this book show forcibly that over 20 years

of operations the Spitfire's profile has altered little, despite the many engine and armament changes it underwent in that time. This surely was proof of the soundness of R J Mitchell's design. Indeed, she retained to the end of her active life 'a beautifully proportioned body' familiar worldwide to a host of admirers.

Which was the supreme mark of the Spitfire? There is disagreement among fighter pilots on this issue, but for me the Spitfire LF Mk IXC takes the prize, embodying as it did the attributes of increased power and a greatly improved rate of climb, without in anyway destroying the handling capabilities – always a fine balance between power and manoeuvrability at all levels. Certainly the introduction of the LF IXC in 1943 tilted the balance between the two main combatants. On the German side the formidable Fw 190 had ruled the roost for the past year, and whilst the Spitfire F Mk IXC then in service disputed this supremacy, it was the later IXC with the Merlin 66 engine which eventually occupied the perch, and held onto it until victory was achieved.

I commend *Spitfire – Flying Legend* to all World War 2 enthusiasts – indeed I go further and suggest that it should be seen and read by the public at large for it illustrates a concept in aircraft design which was to prove a decisive factor in aerial warfare, and one of which we British should be justly proud. The fact that the text should be supported by such outstanding illustrations makes the publication a very worthwhile read. Certainly its contents span the interest of all age groups.

Alan Deere

AIR COMMODORE
ALAN DEERE DSO, OBE, DFC
MAY • 1995

(Sadly, Alan Deere died four months after writing this foreword following a long battle with cancer)

Air Commodore C R Spink CBE FIMgt RAF
Senior Air Staff Officer

Headquarters No 11 Group
Royal Air Force
Bentley Priory

Air Commodore Al Deere has in just a few words provided a compelling foreword to this book on the Spitfire - indeed in the final analysis it is only men of his ilk who can make the final judgement on this most famous of fighter aircraft. For it was the pilots of his generation that had to fly and fight the Spitfire in every corner of the World and that air combat was an unforgiving arena that measured men and machine with ruthless impartiality. That the Spitfire gained, and retained, such a special reputation is testimony not only to the brilliance of R J Mitchell, but to the first class production engineers, test pilots and the front line aircrew who nurtured the concept, and developed the aircraft over the war years to meet every new challenge that an inventive enemy could produce. As a schoolboy in Kent during the post war years I would watch the later marks of Spitfire thunder overhead, never dreaming that one day I would actually be privileged to fly several versions of this outstanding aircraft - albeit only on the display circuit. Indeed, it was Air Cdre Deere, then Commandant of Halton, who first told me that I was to start pilot training, a path that was to take me through the early 'all jet' pilot training of the mid 60s. Therefore, I came to the Spitfire at the tail end of my operational flying career after flying such types as the Hunter, Lightning, Phantom and Tornado. To step back in time was a unique experience, and in truth I wondered whether the legend would live up to reality. It did - and more. There is a 'rightness' about the aircraft that gives an instant feeling of being part of the machine - that said, I found my early flights off metalled runways a time for great attention. On concrete the MkII Spitfire with none of its wartime guns can be as skitterish as a race horse. But in the air the grace of the aircraft is matched by the way it handles - I can well understand what a giant leap forward this Spitfire must have been when biplanes were swapped for this elegant but thoroughly workmanlike aircraft. Subsequent flights in the MkV, IX, XI and IXX have not dispelled my early thrill at flying the BBMF MkII P7350. Indeed, even the Griffon engined version, so often accused of not being a 'real' Spitfire, I found had all of the intrinsic qualities that so distinguishes the aircraft. I also found the MkIX a particularly satisfying aircraft to fly with the wonderful 1600 hp Rolls Merlin 66.

In this book John Dibbs has gathered together a wealth of unpublished material that will be of great interest to all. It perpetuates the just reputation of an aircraft that for over half a century has been a symbol of excellence - the Spitfire.

Bentley Priory
June 1995

Cliff Spink

ACKNOWLEDGEMENTS

Many distinguished individuals have given freely of their time during the compilation of this book, and a suitably detailed acknowledgement to them all could probably form a ninth chapter if space permitted! However, it does not, and the authors' collectively apologise if a name or two has been inadvertently omitted from the following list.

First, and foremost, we would like to thank the owners and pilots of the airworthy Spitfires featured in this work, for without their agreement to allow their precious aircraft to be photographed 'on the wing', this book could not have been done. Therefore, hats off to the following organisations;
The Old Flying Machine Company (OFMC)
The Fighter Collection (TFC)
The Aircraft Restoration Company (ARCO)
The Shuttleworth Collection
Dutch Spitfire Flight
Imperial War Museum, Duxford
Solo Enterprises
Frasca Simulation
Historic Flying Limited
Personal Plane Services
The Battle of Britain Memorial Flight

Aircraft don't fly themselves, and if it wasn't for the skills of the following individuals, *Spitfire – Flying Legend* would be just another book on preserved 'warbirds';
Spitfire pilots – Stephen Grey, Nick Grey, Hoof Proudfoot, Paul Bonhomme,
Ray Hanna, Mark Hanna, Alan Walker, Nigel Lamb, Rod Dean, Brian Smith, Steve Noujaim, Andy Gent,
John Romain, Carolyn Grace, Rick Roberts, Dan Griffith, Tony Bianchi, Andy Sephton, Al Sheppard, Rudy Frasca, Charlie Brown, Tim Routsis, Clive Denney and Paul Shenton.
'Photo-ship' pilots – John Romain, Norman Lees, Alan Walker, Susan Toner, Andy Gent, Richard Verril, Edward Haig-Thomas, Mark Hanna and Dan Griffith
Engineers – Peter Rushen, Dave Lees, Dave Payne and the rest of the team at TFC; Roger Shepherd, Steve Kingman, Tim Fahey, Wayne Fuller and Ray Caller at OFMC; and John Romain, Jon Smith, Colin Swann, Bill Kelly and the team at ARCO.

Turning the clock back five decades, or so, we feel privileged to have been able to recount the combat experiences of Raymond Baxter, Pete Brothers, the late Alan Deere, Don Healey, Ron Hitchcock, 'Jimmy' Taylor, 'Sammy' Sampson and George Unwin, all of whom welcomed the authors into their homes with open arms – their respective wives also deserve thanks for having to put up with yet another afternoon of 'line shooting' about the Spitfire!

Thank you also to the publishers at Wingham Press, Hutchinson, Crécy, Faber and Faber, Pan Books and Grub Street for allowing brief extracts to be quoted from the following books, all of which are recommended as essential reading for anyone even remotely interested in the Spitfire, and the men that flew it;
Smoke Trails in the Sky by Sqn Ldr Anthony Bartley DFC and Bar
William Kimber, 1984
Flying Start by Hugh Dundas
Stanley Paul, 1988
The Last Enemy by Richard Hillary
Pan Books edition, 1980
Nine Lives by Air Commodore Alan C Deere DSO, OBE, DFC
Wingham Press edition, 1991
Over-Paid, Over-Sexed and Over-Here by Lt Col James A Goodson and Norman Franks
Wingham Press, 1991
Spitfire Pilot by Flt Lt D M Crook DFC
Faber and Faber, 1942
Spitfire Offensive by Wg Cdr R W F Sampson OBE, DFC and Bar, and Norman Franks
Grub Street, 1994
Fighter Pilot's Summer by Wg Cdr Paul Richey DFC and Bar, and Norman Franks
Grub Street, 1993
Spitfire – A complete fighting history by Dr Alfred Price
Promotional Reprint Company, 1994 edition

We would also like to thank Air Commodore Cliff Spink for his 'scene setting' foreword, which complements the heartfelt words of the late Air Commodore Alan Deere.

On the black and white photographic front, once again the following individuals have sifted through their respective collections of archival material on behalf of Osprey to find just the right shots to grace the pages in this book; Richard Riding and Mick Oakey at *Aeroplane Monthly*, Phil Jarrett, Dr Alfred Price, Bruce Robertson, Jerry Scutts, and Mike Stroud at *Aerospace Publishing* – thanks guys.

Finally, many thanks to Andy Sephton for the use of his 'pilot's notes' from a typical Shuttleworth display, John O'Neill for shedding light on AR213's restoration to airworthiness all those years ago, and Syd Paine for access to his detailed notes on the multifarious marks of Spitfire and Seafire.

We hope you like the finished product now that you have a copy of the offending article in your hands!

AUTHOR'S PREFACE

My quiet obsession with the Spitfire was nurtured in my early years by reading of the exploits of 'The Few', who piloted these small and fragile machines, and along with Fighter Command's Hurricane pilots, repelled the might of the Nazi aerial armada in true 'Boy's Own' fashion way back in 1940.

It is only with the passing of my own years into adulthood that I realised the magnitude of the events in World War 2, the horror of the conflict, and the sacrifice that eventually brought about victory.

The adult heroes of my childhood reading would have been far younger than I stand at this point in my life, when they fought, and often died, for their country, and the awe in which I view them is only the greater.

The Spitfire in its various guises was with them throughout their struggle from day one to the final Axis surrender, and as time has passed 'The Few' of 1940 and beyond have been superseded (*not* replaced) by another 'few' – the 'few' remaining airframes that survive today, and 'the few' that are privileged to either fly, maintain or work alongside them.

I am lucky enough to be in that number, and we now have a different agenda – simply to ensure that new generations remember not to forget.

JOHN DIBBS
DECEMBER • 1995

INTRODUCTION

As much a national hero as Wellington, Nelson or Montgomery, the Supermarine Spitfire has become the most recognisable icon of World War 2 for several generations of Britons. From the throaty growl of its Rolls-Royce Merlin or Griffon to its beautifully tapered elliptical wings, the Spitfire is a true aeronautical thoroughbred. Regarded by many as the saviour of a nation 'in its darkest hour' (try telling that to a veteran Hurricane pilot from the summer of 1940), the Spitfire is without a doubt the most famous combat aircraft ever produced in Britain.

The history of the Spitfire's ancestry through the Supermarine S.5/6 seaplane racers of Schneider Trophy fame and the rather unattractive F.7/30 (Works Type No 224) has been committed to print on numerous occasions over the past 40 years. Therefore, it is not the purpose of this book to tackle the full development and frontline service history of the Supermarine fighter for the umpteenth time, but rather to focus on a number of airworthy survivors of the breed today, and to bring a flavour of the aircraft's wartime deeds to life through a mix of the best archival photography available, interspersed with selective quotes from Spitfire exponents, both past and present.

In 1996, 60 years after Spitfire prototype K5054's first flight on 5 March 1936 (although many historians quote this date, factory test pilot Jeffrey Quill states in his autobiography, *Spitfire*, that the flight took place on the 6th) from Southampton's Eastleigh aerodrome, examples of Reginald J Mitchell's inspired design continue to perpetuate the wartime legend in ever increasing numbers. As this book went to press, 46 airworthy Spitfires of varying marks were regularly taking to the skies, with a further 44 known to be on rebuild to airworthiness. Add these impressive figures to the remaining 94 estimated to be on static exhibition in museums and private collections across the globe, and one begins to appreciate just how many Spitfires were built in the decade between 1938 and 1948 to allow this number of airframes to survive – 20,351 of all marks, to be precise.

As you look through the pages of this volume at

Along with Sir Sydney Camm, CBE, of Hawkers fame, the name Reginald J Mitchell (or 'R J' as he was known to all and sundry at Supermarine) is synonymous with the best of British aeronautical design. In the 21 years he was at Supermarine, he was responsible for designing no less than 24 types of aircraft, ranging from the Navyplane of 1916, through many elegant Schneider Trophy racers of the 1920s and early 30s, to the Spitfire of 1936. From August 1933 onwards Mitchell fought a losing battle with cancer, but this did not deter him from overseeing the progress of Spitfire prototype K5054 from blueprint drawing through to its first flight from Eastleigh aerodrome, near Southampton, on the morning of 5 March 1936. A man of few words, and an inordinate amount of common sense, Reginald J Mitchell died on Friday 11 June 1937 at the age of just 42. K5054 was destined to be the only Spitfire he ever saw fly
(photo via Don Healey)

This 'snapshot' was taken at Eastleigh just hours after K5054's first flight, and its shows some of the principal players involved in ensuring a smooth 'birth' for the futuristic fighter. Leaning with his arms crossed on the fender of 'R J's' Riley Nine is Vickers-Supermarine Chief Test Pilot, Capt J 'Mutt' Summers, OBE, whilst to his left is Maj H J 'Agony' Payn, AFC, technical assistant to Mitchell, who can be seen sitting on the running board. The 'man from the Air Ministry', Stuart Scott-Hall, is to 'R J's' left, the former serving as resident technical officer at Supermarine. Standing opposite the quartet is Flt Lt Jeffrey 'J K Q' Quill, OBE, AFC, assistant test pilot to 'Mutt' Summers

the beautifully restored aircraft captured 'on the wing' by the camera of John Dibbs, it is hard to imagine the graceful Spitfire being locked in mortal combat with an enemy determined to wipe its lithe planform from the sky. Preciously tended by their owners, today's Spitfires are invariably presented in better condition than when they left the Woolston, Westlands or Castle Bromwich factories and arrived at their first squadrons almost six decades ago. No longer do they have to duel with a deadly foe to ensure survival – the adoration of millions the world over has guaranteed their existence for decades to come.

Home for many of today's Spitfire survivors is Duxford, in Cambridgeshire. A former RAF fighter station with a long and illustrious history, the site is now owned by the Imperial War Museum, and has become a recognised Mecca for warbird enthusiasts from across the globe. Appropriately, Duxford was also the first 'home' for the frontline Spitfire, No 19 Sqn, under the command of Sqn Ldr Henry Iliffe Cozens, making history when the premier production Mk I, K9789, was delivered to them from the Supermarine factory at Woolston on 4 August 1938. This event marked the beginning of the second phase of the monoplane re-equipment for Fighter Command's rapidly expanding force, with the first batch of rival Hawker Hurricane Is having gone into service with No 111 Sqn in December 1937 – by the time the first Spitfire Is flew into Duxford two more squadrons had transitioned to Hurricanes.

The significance of the new arrival at Duxford

Then a new shape in the skies over Cambridgeshire, a loose formation of six Spitfire Is from No 19 Sqn formate with a Blenheim for a series of official RAF photographs to be taken on 31 October 1938. The closest machine to the photographer (K9794 – only the eighth production Spitfire ever built) was being flown on this occasion by No 19 Sqn OC, Sqn Ldr H I Cozens. The hastily-painted number 19 on the tails of the Spitfires was added specially for this sortie

was brought into sharp focus the following month when the Munich Crisis threatened the spectre of war in Europe a full year prior to the eventual invasion of Poland – at this stage in Fighter Command's re-equipment plans 12 short months meant the difference between victory and defeat for Britain as a nation.

'Biplane' Fighter Command

Opposing the mighty Luftwaffe at that time were four freshly-converted Hurricane squadrons, the semi-transitioned No 19 Sqn at Duxford on two-bladed Spitfire Is and no less than 23 units equipped with Gauntlets, Gladiators, Demons or Fury IIs. The latter represented the peacetime 'flying club' RAF of the Hendon Air Pageant era, as the most heavily armed of the quartet – the Gladiator – boasted just four .303 in Browning guns, exactly half the firepower of the Hurricane or Spitfire. The speed difference between the monoplane and biplane fighters was just as significant. For example, when No 41 Sqn finally relinquished its last Fury IIs at Catterick and received early production Spitfire Is in their place, pilots experienced a top speed difference of 155 mph, and an associated climb to altitude rate that increased the higher the monoplane fighter was flown – both crucial factors for a frontline interceptor having to scramble at short notice to repel attacking bombers.

This 'revolution' in the cockpit was experienced by many of those who would later form the backbone of Fighter Command during the Battle of Britain, and in the following passages a handful of notable pilots give their first impressions upon transitioning from Gauntlets and Gladiators to the Spitfire in 1939/40.

Wg Cdr George Unwin was a veteran Sergeant pilot with No 19 Sqn at Duxford when the first Spitfire arrived in Cambridgeshire in August 1938;

'I wouldn't say that we were terrified at the prospect of flying the Spitfire for the first time, but we were more than a little apprehensive to say the least, since we had been flying the most gentlemanly of machines in the Gloster Gauntlet since 1935 – the latter was even easier to handle than the RAF's primary training aircraft of the period, the Avro Tutor. It touched down at about 50 mph, possessed no flaps, no hood and had no retractable anything - indeed, the only thing that moved was the throttle! We therefore went straight from this thoroughly familiar machine one day, straight on to the seemingly massive brute of a Spitfire the next, without the aid of even a dual-control trainer.

'However, a lot of our initial fears were soon removed following the display put on over our airfield by Supermarine Test Pilot Jeffrey Quill prior to his delivery of the first Spitfire. This performance would have satisfied any potential pilot of the fighter, and he completed his routine by carrying out a perfect landing just to show us how easy it was.

'Nevertheless, we went about our transition without even a set of pilot's notes in those early days

of 1938. All we possessed was a scrap of paper on which had been scrawled the climbing, diving, cruising and stalling speeds, and that was about it. After the Gauntlet the cockpit seemed to be full of switches and levers, operating things like the flaps and undercarriage that popped open and closed. Indeed, on the first batch of Mk Is which we received, extension and retraction of the gear was achieved through the pumping of a huge lever sited on the right-hand side of the cockpit – you could always tell a Spitfire pilot undergoing his first solo take-off for as he pumped on the lever he would push the control column up and down as well, causing the aircraft to porpoise accordingly! Fortunately, powered undercarriage retraction was installed in the next production run of aircraft.

'First our CO, Sqn Ldr Cozens, went off and successfully performed the unit's inaugural Spitfire flight, followed by the two flight commanders, and then as the senior Sergeant pilot at No 19 Sqn, I became the first NCO to fly the fighter at Duxford. I was a fairly confident pilot by that time, having been on Gauntlets for nearly three years, and I experienced no noticeable problems at all in handling the Spitfire in the air. Indeed, aside from poor old Gordon Sinclair, who pranged K9792 upon landing after his first solo – this was due to a faulty axle stub which sheared off during his roll out – the whole unit completed the transition from Gauntlet to Spitfire in short order.

'Following my successful mastering of the aircraft, I was heavily involved in completing the development trials of the fighter, as in those days the RAF hadn't a set up like today's Boscombe Down evaluation centre, where a new type is "wrung out" prior to it being issued to the frontline. We had to put 500 hours on a single aircraft as quickly as possible in order to formulate a rudimentary maintenance

Sadly devoid of serials, but nevertheless wearing No 19 Sqn's short-lived 'WZ' codes, pre-war two-colour roundels and no fin flash, this impressive line up of 11 Spitfires Is was the sight that greeted the Fleet Street press upon their arrival at RAF Duxford on 4 May 1939. This was the first facility organised by the RAF for journalists and photographers to view the new Supermarine fighter in close-up in frontline service, and amongst the throng who flocked to the Cambridgeshire air station was the legendary Charles E Brown, who took this shot. From his elevated viewpoint Brown has captured the groundcrews readying the machines for a flypast of Duxford, which was the culmination of the Press Day. Note the mix of canopy styles, and that the Mk I in the foreground appears to be the only Spitfire lacking an individual letter code

Sgt George 'Grumpy' Unwin and *Flash*, his Alsation, pose by a chocked K9798 (note the serial painted in black and white immediately beneath the two-bladed prop boss) at Duxford in late 1938. Ironically, of the 48 different Spitfires George flew with No 19 Sqn between August 1938 and December 1940, this machine was not amongst them! This may be due to the fact that K9798 only enjoyed a seven-month life in the frontline, being reduced to a static training tool following a wheels up landing at Duxford on 18 April 1939. It had only flown a total of 168.30 hours prior to its accident *(George Unwin)*

schedule for all Fighter Command units to adopt. A team of five pilots consisting of the CO, the two flight commanders, Flt Sgt Harry Steere and myself were selected to fly our very first Spitfire – K9789 – until it reached this milestone. To achieve 500 hours it flew all hours of daylight, but never at night because we were fearful it may get damaged upon landing. Due to a rash of minor accidents with the early Hurricanes "Treble One" Squadron were still trying to achieve a similar figure down at Northolt on a single airframe, having had their fighters a full nine months before we received our first Spitfire!

'We sailed straight through with K9789, and once the novelty had worn off the CO stepped down from the evaluation team and the two flight commanders found that they couldn't fly during their lunch hour, so it was left to Harry Steere and myself to perform the bulk of the sorties. The only problem we encountered during the trial occurred at the end of the last trip in front of the whole squadron as Harry taxied the machine in after landing. Despite having two green lights in the cockpit denoting that the gear was locked down, K9789 experienced a freak unlocking of the mechanism and the port oleo began to retract in front of us. Fortunately the groundcrew saw his predicament in time and dashed across the field like jack rabbits, dived under the offending wing and propped it up until the propeller had stopped.

'A piece of rope was quickly slung around the legs, the right one holding up the left, and the Spitfire was duly towed in to the dispersal area – even with this last minute hiccup we had still completed our 500 hours before the Hurricane boys!

'Aside from the performance attributes of the Spitfire over the Gauntlet, the aeroplane also boasted a radio that worked so well that you could actually hear what people were saying. The original TR.9 H/F wireless in our biplanes was virtually useless over a distance greater than five miles from the transmitter as the atmospherics obliterated the signal – I really don't know why we bothered carrying it to be honest. The Spitfire was equipped with the much improved VHF TR.9D version, and due to our greater ceilings, the distance over which communication could be achieved was astounding. During the 500-hour trials, in order to avoid boredom during the hour-and-a-half-long sorties I would literally cruise all over the UK at 30,000 ft and periodically call up for a bearing and actually get one in return – this really was a novelty!'

Alan Deere

The late Air Commodore Alan Deere was a Pilot Officer with No 54 Sqn at Hornchurch when he traded his recently camouflaged Gladiator for a brand new two-pitch de Havilland three-bladed Spitfire I in March 1939. Although his initial transition to the Supermarine fighter went smoothly, his lack of familiarity with one of its more advanced features soon caught him out, as he relates in this passage from his classic autobiography, *Nine Lives;*

'On March 6th, 1939, I flew my first Spitfire, an aircraft very little different from the later marks with

which the RAF finished the war. In many respects, however, the Mk I was a nicer aircraft, and certainly much lighter than subsequent Marks which became over-powered and over-weighted with armour plating and cannons. The transition from slow biplanes to the faster monoplanes was effected without fuss, and in a manner of weeks we were nearly as proficient on Spitfires as we had been on Gladiators.

'Two days after my first flight in a Spitfire, I was sent down to Eastleigh airfield to collect a new aircraft (K9886) from the Supermarine Works where the Spitfire was produced.

'The weather was pretty bad for the trip and I had the greatest difficulty finding Hornchurch. Such was my relief when I did find the airfield that I couldn't resist a quick beat-up, very much frowned on in those days. I noticed as I taxied towards the squadron hangar after landing that there was more than the normal complement of pilots to greet me. I was soon to learn why. Not only had I committed the sin of beating up the airfield, I had neglected to change from fine to coarse pitch after take-off from Eastleigh with the result that there was a great deal more noise than normal on my quite small beat-up and, worse still, the brand new Spitfire was smothered in oil thrown out by the over-revving engine.

'A very red-faced Pilot Officer faced an irate Flt Lt "Bubbles" Love, my flight commander, who was

These Mk Is were amongst the first batch of 310 Spitfires ordered (308 delivered) by the Air Ministry, and built by Supermarine at their Woolston plant between May 1938 and September 1939. Very much 'hand-built' in true British aeronautical tradition, these early aircraft were somewhat 'over-engineered' by tradesmen still struggling to come to grips with the new technologies embodied in the Spitfire. Therefore, they took longer to complete than similar aircraft built at 'shadow factories' two years later. This shot was taken on 23 January 1939

This Spitfire IA is having its eight 0.303 in Brownings test fired and harmonised at the gun butts on the edge of an undisclosed fighter station in the late summer of 1940. The empty shell casings can be clearly seen falling onto the tarmac from the cartridge chutes on the undersurface of the wing. Each of the Mk IA's eight guns fitted in the standard 'A' wing boasted up to 300 rounds per weapon, which usually consisted of ball, incendiary and armour-piercing ammunition. Despite the Browning's excellent rate of fire (about 17 rounds per second per gun at best, or a combined 150 rounds for all eight Brownings firing at once) and light weight, its ammunition was only of rifle calibre size, which often proved ineffective against heavily-armoured Heinkel, Junkers and Dornier bombers in 1940 *(via Bruce Robertson)*

decent enough to let the matter rest at a good "ticking-off".'

For many pilots who volunteered, or were called up, during September 1939, the Spitfire was the first frontline type they encountered after completing their flying training. Although these aeronautical tyros lacked experience when compared with pre-war regulars like George Unwin and Alan Deere, the inherent 'airworthiness' of the Supermarine design allowed most to feel at home from the word go. Amongst the ranks of *ab initio* Fighter Command pilots was the then Plt Off David Crook, who had seen limited flying training with his local auxiliary unit – No 609 'West Riding' Sqn – in the pre-war months, and who had been sent to No 6 FTS for further tuition upon being called up in August 1939. He returned to No 609 Sqn, then stationed at Drem, in Scotland, in May 1940, and he noted his first impressions of the Spitfire in the following extract from his wartime novel, *Spitfire Pilot*;

'The next day I did my first trip in a Spitfire. I had waited for this moment for nearly two years, and when it came it was just as exciting as I had always expected.

'Having mastered the cockpit drill, I got in and taxied out on to the aerodrome, sat there for one moment to check that everything was OK, and then opened up to full throttle. The effect took my breath away. The engine opened up with a great smooth roar, the Spitfire leapt forward like a bullet and tore madly across the aerodrome, and before I had realised quite what had happened I was in the air. I felt as though the machine was completely out of control and running away with me. However, I collected my scattered wits, raised the undercarriage, and put the airscrew into coarse pitch, and then looked round for the aerodrome, which to my astonishment I saw was already miles behind.

'After a few minutes' cruising round I realised that this fearsome beast was perhaps not quite so formidable as I had thought in that first breathless minute, so I decided to try a landing. This came off reasonably satisfactorily, and I took off again, feeling much more sure of myself. So I climbed up to a good height and played about in the clouds in this superb new toy and did a few gentle dives to 400 mph, which gave me a tremendous thrill. Altogether I was almost light-headed with exhilaration when I landed at the end of an hour's flight, and I felt that I could ask nothing more of life.

'Actually, once you have done a few hours' flying in a Spitfire and become accustomed to the great power and speed, then it is an extraordinarily easy machine to fly and it is absolutely marvellous for aerobatics. Practically everybody who has flown a Spitfire thinks it is the most marvellous aircraft ever built, and I am no exception to the general rule. I grew to like it more than any other machine I have flown. It is so small and compact and neat, yet it possesses devastating fire power, and is still probably the best and the fastest fighter in the world. The new fighters which will soon be coming into service will have to do very well to equal the Spitfire's amazing record of success.'

Having survived the Battle of Britain and several years as an instructor, Flt Lt David Crook was eventually killed in a flying accident in a Spitfire IX in December 1944.

Like Crook, Sqn Ldr Anthony Bartley also joined the RAF in 1939, and upon completion of his FTS course later that year was posted to No 92 Sqn, where he initially flew the 'dreaded' Blenheim IF night-fighter. However, March 1940 brought a change of type as the first Spitfires arrived at Tangmere, and his initial impressions are graphically expressed in the following extract taken from his detailed autobiography, *Smoke Trails in the Sky*;

'On March 6th 1940, three weeks before my 21st birthday, No 92 Sqn was re-equipped with Spitfires. The bogey men of Blenheims and black nights had dawned into horizons of dawn sunlight and blue skies.

'One of the unique and most alarming experi-

The eight guns, and associated ammunition bays, of the Mk I/IA's 'A' wing were covered by 22 panels secured by 150 turn buttons. It was estimated that a proficient four-man re-arming team could turn a Spitfire around in 30 minutes. This Mk I of No 602 'City of Glasgow' Sqn was photographed at Drem in April 1940

This shot, taken on the same visit to No 602 Sqn at Drem as the previous view, shows the pilot fastening his helmet chin strap prior to climbing aboard his already idling Spitfire I *(via Jerry Scutts)*

ences in one's life must surely be to find oneself alone in an aeroplane for the very first time, completely dependent upon oneself to get back to mother earth. In air terminology, this is called 'Soloing'. My second most exciting experience was to fly a Spitfire for the first time. It was like driving a racing car after an Austin . . . riding a racehorse, after a hack. It just didn't seem to want to slow down. When one pulled back on the throttle, it took a long time to take effect on its speed.

'In contrast to the Blenheim, the Spitfire was the perfection of a flying machine designed to combat and destroy its enemy. It had no vices, carried great fire power, and a Rolls-Royce motor which very rarely stopped. An aerodynamic masterpiece, and a joy to fly'

Another noted pilot who fell in love with the Spitfire from the moment he saw it was Grp Capt Hugh Dundas, who sadly passed away as this book was being compiled. He first flew the aircraft whilst serving as a young Pilot Officer with No 616 'South Yorkshire' Sqn at Leconfield on 13 March 1940, and in his gripping book, *Flying Start*, he wholeheartedly praises the machine;

'There is something Wagnerian about facets of the Spitfire story, the more so since it is certainly true that there never was a plane so loved by pilots, combining as it did sensitive yet docile handling characteristics with deadly qualities as a fighting machine. Lovely to look at, delightful to fly, the Spitfire became the pride and joy of thousands of young men from practically every country in what, then, constituted the free world. Americans raved about her and wanted to have her: Poles were seduced by her; the Free French undoubtedly wrote love songs about her. And the Germans were envious of her.

Unaware that (officially at least) the Battle of Britain was now over, the entire flying complement of No 41 Sqn look happy enough in this informal group shot taken at RAF Hornchurch in November 1940. The central figure in the front row is Sqn Ldr Don Finlay, who led the squadron from September 1940 through to August of the following year. Prior to assuming command of the unit he had briefly led No 54 Sqn, also on Spitfires, and again from Hornchurch. A pre-war pilot who had joined the RAF on a Permanent Commission in 1935, Finlay completed two tours with Nos 17 and 54 Sqns prior to the outbreak of war – he had also won a silver medal in the hurdles at the 1936 Berlin Olympics! He finished the war an ace with five kills *(via Bruce Robertson)*

One of Fighter Command's most publicised Spitfire pilots during the early years of the war was the spectacularly successful Dubliner, Brendan Eamonn Fergus 'Paddy' Finucane – here he is seen at the left of the photo carrying out a post-sortie de-brief with Australian pilots from No 452 (RAAF) Sqn in 1941. He first served notice of his potential whilst with No 65 Sqn during the Battle of Britain, where he claimed two Bf 109Es destroyed, a further two as probables and a fifth fighter damaged during two days of frenetic action from Manston in the lead up to the Luftwaffe's *Eagle Day* – 13 August 1940. By the time of his death on 15 July 1942, he had claimed 26 kills and 8 probables, 6 shared kills and a single shared probable, and 8 damaged *(via Jerry Scutts)*

'Little did I know as I taxied in from that first Spitfire flight that I would not taxi in from my last until late in 1949. We went through the war together, with only a year's separation when, in 1942, I temporarily – and not very happily – flirted with the Typhoon.

'In all those years no misfortune which came our way was ever the fault of the Spitfire. Owing to the loss of my second log book – the first ran up to the end of July 1942 – I do not know exactly how many hundreds of hours I spent in a Spitfire's cockpit, over sea, desert and mountains, in storm and sunshine, in conditions of great heat and great cold, by day and by night, on the deadly business of war and in the pursuit of pleasure. I do know that the Spitfire never let me down and that on the occasions when we got into trouble together the fault was invariably mine.'

One of the most eloquent, and honest, appraisals of the feelings experienced by a young pilot encountering the Spitfire for the first time came from Richard Hillary, who was posted to No 603 'City of Edinburgh' Sqn at Dyce, in Scotland, in June 1940, following conversion training at Aston Down with No 5 OTU;

'And we learned finally to fly the Spitfire.

'I faced the prospect with some trepidation. Here for the first time was a machine in which there was no chance of making a dual circuit as a preliminary. I must solo right off, and in the fastest machine in the world.

'One of the squadron pilots took me up for a couple of trips in a Miles Master, the British trainer most similar to a Spitfire in characteristics.

'I was put through half an hour's instrument flying under the hood in a Harvard, and then I was ready. At least I hoped I was ready. Kilmartin (Flg Off John Kilmartin, a Hurricane ace of the Battle of France, Ed.), a slight, dark-haired Irishman in charge

of our Flight, said, "Get your parachute and climb in. I'll show you the cockpit before you go off".

'He sauntered over to the machine, and I found myself memorising every detail of his appearance with the clearness of a condemned man on his way to the scaffold – the chin sunk into the folds of a polo-sweater, the leather pads on the elbows, and the string-darned hole in the seat of the pants. He caught my look of anxiety and grinned.

"Don't worry; you'll be surprised how easy she is to handle."

'I hoped so.

'The Spitfires stood in two lines outside "A" Flight pilots' room. The dull grey-brown of the camouflage could not conceal the clear-cut beauty, the wicked simplicity of their lines. I hooked up my parachute and climbed awkwardly into the low cockpit. I noticed how small was my field of vision. Kilmartin swung himself on to a wing and started to run through the instruments. I was conscious of his voice, but heard nothing of what he said. I was to fly a Spitfire. It was what I had most wanted through all the long dreary months of training. If I could fly a Spitfire, it would be worth it. Well, I was about to achieve my ambition and felt nothing. I was numb, neither exhilarated nor scared. I noticed the white enamel undercarriage handle. "Like a lavatory plug", I thought.

'"What did you say?"

'Kilmartin was looking at me and I realised I had spoken aloud. I pulled myself together.

'"Have you got all that?" he asked.

'"Yes, sir."

'"Well off you go then. About four circuits and bumps. Good luck!"

'He climbed down.

'I taxied slowly across the field, remembering suddenly what I had been told: that the Spitfire's prop was long and that it was therefore inadvisable to push the stick too far forward when taking off; that the Spitfire was not a Lysander (Hillary's previous type, Ed.) and that any hard application of the brake when landing would result in a somersault and immediate transfer to a Battle squadron. Because of the Battle's lack of power and small armament this was regarded by everyone as the ultimate disgrace.

'I ran quickly through my cockpit drill, swung the nose into the wind, and took off. I had been flying automatically for several minutes before it dawned on me that I was actually in the air, undercarriage retracted and half-way round the circuit without incident. I turned into wind and hauled up my seat, at the same time pushing back the hood. I came in low, cut the engine just over the boundary hedge, and floated down on all three points. I took off again. Three more times I came round for a perfect landing. It was too easy. I waited across wind for a minute and watched with satisfaction several machines bounce badly as they came in. Then I taxied rapidly back to the hangars and climbed out nonchalantly. Noel (Plt Off Noel Agazarian, who later became an ace that summer with No 609 Sqn, Ed.), who had not yet soloed, met me.

'"How was it?" he said.

'I made a circle of approval with my thumb and forefinger.

'"Money for old rope", I said.

'I didn't make another good landing for a week.'

Australian-born Richard Hillary flew into battle with No 603 Sqn from Hornchurch until he was shot down in flames on 2 September 1940. Dreadfully burnt during his escape from his doomed Spitfire, he spent over a year in hospital, during which time he wrote the classic novel *The Last Enemy*, from which the extract was taken. He retrained as a nightfighter pilot in 1942, but was

Although often published as the classic image of the Battle of Britain, this atmospheric view of No 610 'County of Chester' Sqn out on a Channel convoy patrol from Gravesend was actually taken in early June 1940. The unit had seen much action over France following its posting south to Biggin Hill from Prestwick on 10 May, and the lessons learnt in combat are reflected in the loose line-astern formations flown by two of the three sections seen in this view – only the closest flight has adopted a pre-war 'vic'. Part of the latter formation is Mk IA L1043/ 'DW-O', which first flew on 3 July 1939, and was initially issued to No 19 Maintenance Unit (MU). It stayed here until being sent as an attrition replacement to No 610 Sqn, then at Acklington, in December 1939. It fought throughout May and June with the unit, before being passed on to No 266 Sqn soon after this shot was taken. In September the unit re-equipped with Mk IIAs, and it was relegated to Training Command. L1043 served briefly with No 7 OTU, before being sent to No 57 OTU where it was written off in an accident on 24 September. 'DW-K' (Mk IA P9495) first flew on 4 April 1940, and was then issued to No 8 MU – from here it went to No 610 Sqn on 2 June 1940. On the morning of 12 August the unit was scrambled to intercept nine Bf 109Es of II./JG 52 near New Romney. In the ensuing melée two Messerschmitts and a Spitfire were lost, with a further three No 610 Sqn machines being damaged – one of the latter was P9495 which, despite landing back at Biggin Hill, was so badly hit by cannon fire that it was struck off charge 12 days later

tragically killed in a flying accident in a Blenheim in January 1943.

Eagle Squadrons

Aviators from most Allied nations got to fly the Spitfire, with the American pilots of the elite Eagle Squadrons being amongst the most praiseworthy of the type. Col Jim Goodson was one of the first 'Yanks' in the RAF, and he describes his feelings for the machine – particularly in relation to its stablemate the Hurricane, which he initially flew in combat in early 1941 – in the following passage taken from his eloquently titled autobiography *Over-Paid, Over-Sexed and Over Here*;

'I write about the Hurricane with admiration and affection, tinged with a little sorrow. In a way, it was sad that this great old war-horse was put in the shade by its successor. The beautiful Spitfire immediately took the limelight and even took the credit for winning the Battle of Britain, in which there were far more Hurricanes involved than Spitfires.

'Of course, the Spitfire was a lovely plane, combining speed, manoeuvrability and beauty. But let's not forget the old Hurricane, as those of us who flew it never will. She forgave many mistakes that the Spitfire wouldn't, both in the air and on the ground, and in the early days, when we took to the air with so little experience, we needed a lot of forgiveness.

'The Spit was a little bitch on the ground. The long nose blocking your forward vision completely meant that you had to constantly weave right and left, and if you took too long before taking off, you could lose your brakes entirely through lack of air, or even overheat the engine. The narrow landing-gear also made it prone to ground-looping on landing or take-off if the field was uneven.

'In the Hurricane, you could trundle around on the ground as you liked, and you had to be really ham-fisted to ground loop it. In the air, too, the Hurricane was much steadier than the Spitfire. "Johnnie" Johnson's first comment after being in combat in a Spitfire was "The Hurricane was a much better gun platform".

'I knew exactly what he meant. The very first time I got onto the tail of an enemy plane in a Spitfire, I missed him. It wasn't because I opened fire before I was in range, or anything like that; I should have blown him to bits, and would have if I'd been flying a Hurricane. But the firing button on the Spitfire was on the top of the control column and the Spitfire was so sensitive that, when I pressed the trigger, the nose pitched down and I missed the target.

'The same applied on landing. The Hurricane just came in, plunked itself down and rolled to a stop. One always knew a pilot who had just transferred to Spitfires – he bounced three times down the runway! Nevertheless, the Spitfire was a lady, and everyone who flew her had a love affair with her – she was that kind of lady.

'When you got used to the Spit, you became part of it. You didn't aim your guns, you aimed yourself. The controls were so sensitive you didn't have the impression of forcing the plane to follow your will; it was as if your will was automatically converted into action. So little effort was needed to handle her that one was inclined to move the plane rather than move one's body.'

The common thread running throughout these first-hand accounts is that R J Mitchell's final design was a pilot's machine right from the start. It allowed the novice of 1939/40 to feel confident in his ability to acquit himself well in combat with the all-conquering Luftwaffe, whilst equally reassuring the seasoned veteran that his skills accrued over the years on various biplane fighters would be honed to an unprecedented level once the fight began.

Just to temper all this adoration, the following – and final – quote in this introduction to the Spitfire comes from Battle of France Hurricane ace Paul Richey, whose original wartime work, *Fighter Pilot*, has become a standard text for historians studying the RAF's doomed efforts on the continent in 1940. In his second book, *Fighter Pilot's Summer*, compiled following his death in 1989 by noted historian Norman Franks, Richey discusses in meticulous detail going back on ops on Spitfire Vs for the first time in the spring of 1941 after evacuating France almost a year before;

'After tea that evening, the Bishop (No 609 Sqn ace Flg Off John Bisdee, Ed.) took me up to the aerodrome in his little Austin to show me over the controls of a Spitfire. Having been a Hurricane pilot for two years, I knew little about the Spitfire and had seldom even seen one. I also had the Hurricane pilot's conversion: I never hoped to fly a better fighter.

'This was perhaps understandable for though an older machine than the Spitfire, the Hurricane had been well tried in peace-time, had done magnificently in the Battles of France and Britain and had shot down far more enemy aircraft than the Spitfire. Besides, what made most difference was that my own battles had been fought in it, so that I had every con-

Some Spitfires lasted a matter of days in the frontline, whilst others kept on flying until they were deemed to be obsolescent and duly sold for scrap. Spitfire IIA P8147 was amongst the latter, having been 'bought' by the people of the city of Norwich, whose name it proudly wore beneath the canopy on the port side. It was initially issued to No 65 'East India' Sqn on 29 April 1941, and spent the next four months flying mundane defensive patrols over the North Sea from Kirton-in-Lindsey, near Lincoln. Following a spell at Westlands, where undisclosed modification work was carried out, P8147 was issued on 11 December to the Polish-manned No 308 'City of Krakow' Sqn, who had just been posted for a rest to Woodvale, near Liverpool, following a long spell on offensive sweeps from Northolt flying Mk VBs. By 4 February 1942 P8147 had started its final stint with a frontline unit, the recently-formed No 350 'Belgian' Sqn flying it in combat from Warmwell and Debden in April. P8147's combat career finally ended the following month, however, and it was passed to a succession of second-line training units. This well-worn Mk IIA was finally struck off charge on 30 November 1944 *(via Bruce Robertson)*

fidence in it and I was thoroughly at home in one and "as one piece".

'I therefore approached my first Spitfire with a certain amount of distaste. I had seen them flying and admitted I had seen few prettier aircraft. But on the ground, to my biased eye, the Spit looked knock-kneed, flimsy and rather silly. It lacked the air of robust strength of my beloved Hurry. However, I had to admit its superior lines in flight. Then she really did look a thoroughbred.

'"Here we are", said Bish, as he jumped up on the port wing root and slid back the hood. "You'd better get in – you'll be able to see better." I clambered in. The cockpit felt too small and cramped.

'"Now, let's see", said Bish. "Here's your throttle, the petrol cocks here, up for on; mixture control and airscrew control. Undercarriage here – lever right up and in the slot for up, where it is now for down. Lights over the indicators there. Emergency undercarriage release – this lever on the CO_2 bottle here. Flaps here – forward for starboard, back for port. Radiator shutter here – back for shut. Switches: main engine switches, starter-mag, pitot-heating, camera-gun, IFF, pip-squeak, reflector-sight, generator.

'"You won't want night flying stuff now so I won't bother you with it. R/T here – four buttons, one for each frequency. Call-signs and ground-stations you know. Oxygen – tap here, regulator there. Rudder adjustment – those things down there. Seat adjustment – this lever here. Windscreen de-icer here. And emergency hood release here.

'"Instruments are standard; blind flying with artificial horizon, turn and bank, rate of climb and ascent, gyro-compass, sensitive altimeter and so on. Compass down there, glycol temperature-gauge, oil temperature gauge and oil pressure gauge here: boost pressure gauge and rev counter here; air pressure gauge between your feet. I think that's the lot. If I've forgotten anything I expect you'll find it. Oh, yes – the gun button is here."

'As we walked over to get my flying-helmet from the Dispersal Hut the Bish gave me one or two tips, regarding boost pressures, speeds for lowering undercarriage and flaps, trimming for take-off, starting up and so on. Then, once more seated in the cockpit, I buckled on my parachute and fighting harnesses, closed the door, started up, ran the engine up, waved the chocks and airmen away and taxied out to the downwind end of the runway in use.

'I flew three circuits and landings, and some mild aerobatics, none of which I enjoyed. I found the elevators too sensitive, the ailerons too stiff, the nose too long and too high, the cockpit cramped and the vision restricted. The only thing I liked was the layout of the cockpit. The aeroplane flew alright but the thought of fighting in it I relished not at all! I taxied in feeling both disappointed and worried, wondering whether it was the aeroplane or me that was wrong.

Micky (Sqn Ldr Michael Robinson, both No 609 Sqn OC and at that point the unit's leading ace, Ed.) was there to meet me. "How d'you like it?" he asked with a smile.

'"Not much", I said glumly.

'"Don't worry, old boy", he said. "I felt exactly the same after I'd come off Hurricanes, but after I'd done about 20 hours I wouldn't change it for anything. You'll see. Come on we'll go and have a drink."

'This was slightly reassuring, for Micky was an experienced and exceptionally fine pilot and I naturally respected his judgement.'

Despite Paul Richey's lack of enthusiasm for the Spitfire upon their first meeting, he nevertheless went on to complete 61 missions in Mk IIAs and VBs during his tour, which lasted from April through to August 1941. In that time he claimed two Bf 109Es confirmed destroyed and one Bf 109F probable, as well as damaging six Bf 109Fs. He finally conceded many years after the war that the Spitfire was indeed an effective fighter, although at the same time clearly spelling out its faults;

'Every aeroplane is a compromise between what the designer wants out of it and the operational needs. Some have good climb, at the expense of something else – strength probably – because they have to make it light and some have manoeuvrability at the expense of speed, because it won't manoeuvre well if it's a very fast aeroplane. The Spitfire was a good compromise; it had its faults, like all aeroplanes and it had very sensitive elevators. However, the ailerons were rather soggy. So in some aircraft you could whip very quickly into a turn but in others you couldn't. But the Spitfire made up for it in many other ways.'

Indeed it did!

This marvellous photo shows a clutch of Eagle Squadron pilots looking on as Flg Off Jim Daley, from Amarillo, Texas, describes to No 121 Sqn's intelligence officer at North Weald just how he tackled an enemy fighter less than an hour before. The date of this shot is likely to be 8 March 1942, as Daley tasted his first combat success on this day – he damaged an Fw 190 on a sweep south of Dunkirk whilst flying Spitfire VB AD139. However, the presence of the pilot to his right (9-kill ace Peter Powell, who had been OC of No 121 Sqn until January 1942, when he was promoted to lead the Hornchurch Wing) suggests perhaps an earlier date

CHAPTER ONE

THE EARLY MARKS

Spitfire Mk IA AR213 and Mk IIA P7350

Flight Sergeant George 'Grumpy' Unwin
No 19 Sqn
August 1936 to December 1940

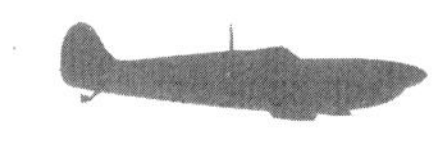

'We (No 19 Sqn) had only barely started our operational conversion at Duxford from Gauntlet IIs to Spitfire Is when the Munich Crisis blew up in September 1938. We received a message from No 12 Group HQ to be prepared for action, and responded by standing readiness with nine Gauntlets and three Spitfires. I had one of the latter, as did my chum Flt Sgt Harry Steere, which meant that two of the three "senior pilots" – based on hours flown on type – on the Supermarine fighter at this time were NCOs!

'God knows what would have happened if we had all been scrambled off to meet the enemy together – this thought often crossed our minds during the tense winter of 1938/39, until the last of the Gauntlets was finally replaced the following February – it took until the end of 1938 to receive our full complement of 16 Spitfires from Supermarines, as they were only being delivered at the rate of about one per week.

'We never actually indulged in any dogfighting between Spitfires and Gauntlets during the squadron's conversion period, and once fully equipped with the new fighter we refrained from "taking on" rival Hurricane units as well. This was despite the fact that we had endured regular airfield "beat-ups" by No 111 Sqn in their brand new Hurricane Is from early 1938 onwards.'

Duxford was a favourite 'target' for two reasons – 1.) No 19 Sqn had been the premier fighter squadron in the RAF for much of the 1930s, winning the Sir Philip Sassoon Flight Attack Challenge Trophy and numerous aerobatics/display flying awards, as well as being chosen to usher firstly the Gauntlet and then the Spitfire into frontline service; and 2.) Sqn Ldr Harry Broadhurst, an ex-Flight Commander with No 19 Sqn, who was partly responsible for the unit garnering much of this glory due to his exceptional flying skills and unmatched marksmanship, had assumed command of 'Treble One' in January 1939.

'As soon as we had 12 Spitfires on strength, and a similar number of pilots experienced on type, our CO, Sqn Ldr Henry Iliffe Cozens, took us over to "Treble One's" airfield at RAF Northolt and we thoroughly "beat up" their dispersal – so much so that we never saw No 111 Sqn again.

'One of the main complaints that we had at No 19 Sqn about our first batch of Spitfires was the extraordinarily long take-off roll the fighter boasted with the original fixed-pitch two-bladed wooden propeller, particularly when compared with the nimble and light Gauntlet. The beautifully-crafted prop had been optimised to give its best performance at both high speed and medium to high altitude – the Spitfire was a fighter interceptor after all. However, at Duxford we only had a grass strip that was 800 to 900 yards long, and to further compound the squadron's initial problems, following the delivery of

our first two Spitfires in early August, we had no wind of any note to assist our take-offs until late September!

'We had to resort to taxying as near to the leeward hedge as possible. The brakes were then applied whilst you opened the throttle flat out, and once the RPM gauge was showing constant revs, the brakes were released and the Spitfire began its seemingly endless take-off run. Even with this time-consuming pre-flight procedure, which would have been totally impractical in a proper wartime scramble, the fighter barely cleared the hawthorn hedge at the far end of the grass strip.'

Fortunately, Supermarine were quick to realise that their product was being hindered by such a device, and the interim de Havilland two-pitch 'bracket' type propeller was adopted, although this in turn brought with it problems, with pilots forgetting to select fine pitch for take-off on the cockpit control box above the throttle and duly running out of airfield – the Spitfire accelerated too slowly in coarse pitch to achieve take-off speed.

One such accident directly attributable to wrong pitch selection befell no less an RAF legend than Douglas Bader – and resulted in George Unwin receiving the appellation 'Grumpy', which has stuck with him till this day. Upon his readmittance to the RAF, Flg Off Bader had been posted to No 19 Sqn in February 1940 to gain experience on the Spitfire, prior to being posted to No 222 Sqn as a Flight Commander.

Detailed to carry out a convoy patrol, he was leading a three-ship formation take-off from No 19 Sqn's satellite field at Horsham St Faith on 31 March when his Spitfire (K9858) crashed through the boundary hedge and cartwheeled across a ploughed field. It was a total write-off. Taking off slightly downwind directly from dispersal, Bader's wingmen realised their leader's error in having failed to select fine pitch, and managed to open their throttles and just clear the hedgerow – Douglas became aware of his error at about the same time, and hit the appropriate button on his prop selector control, but it was too late.

He escaped without a scratch, although his 'tin legs' were also Category E, just like his near-new Spitfire. George Unwin takes up the story;

'Days after Bader's prang I was detached to Horsham with members of my flight, and Douglas persisted in continually filing his recently arrived replacement tin legs, in order to get them working just as he liked them. I remonstrated with him after enduring as much of the scratching and scraping as I physically could whilst trying to get some sleep. The film *Snow White and the Seven Dwarfs* was showing at that time, and Bader simply replied, "Oh shut up Grumpy". From then on that was my nickname.'

Battle Formation

As with all other Fighter Command units in early 1940, No 19 Sqn was still performing patrols in unweildy battle formations made up of four 'vics' of

BELOW This view of No 19 Sqn's two-bladed Spitfires was also taken on the press day held at Duxford on 4 May 1939. Note the broad chord of the fixed-pitch wooden propeller, and the differing camouflage patterns applied to the first three machines, particularly around the nose – the camouflage pattern of the 'T'-coded Spitfire in the foreground denotes that its serial (obscured by the censors) ended with an odd number. Fighter Command had two main schemes which were factory applied to aircraft depending on whether the machine in question had been allocated a serial that ended in an odd or even number. Evens wore the 'A' scheme and odds the 'B' scheme, but both consisted of dark green and dark earth upper surfaces, and in the months prior to the outbreak of war, half black and half white undersurfaces

three aircraft. These textbook routines had their roots firmly fixed in the inter-war biplane era, and the Spitfire brought a new dimension to the whole concept of offensive patrols from a pure airmanship standpoint for the man in the cockpit, as George Unwin explains;

'Performing close formation patrols for any period of time was tiring, and in the Spitfire you couldn't just pop your head out of the cockpit to check your position, relative to your leader or wingman. Conversely, you didn't have a ruddy great radial engine in front of you, a top wing blanking off much of your upward vision, and struts and bracing wire restricting your lateral outlook. However, the big advantage with the Spitfire as far as we were concerned wasn't the improved visibility, but rather the in-cockpit comfort, as with our new fighter we could stay warm at any height!

'In the Gauntlet – which had a higher ceiling thanks to its biplane configuration – during our once-weekly battle formation exercise, which often reached altitudes of 35,000 ft, you just got colder, and colder, until you had no feeling left in your limbs at all. That was fine until you began to descend – and thaw out. It was agony regaining the feeling in your fingers and toes, and despite wearing three layers of clothing, plus the occasional flirtation with heated suits, the only thing that really cured the problem was the advent of the monoplane fighter, with its enclosed cockpit! In the Spitfire I usually just wore my standard uniform, with a *Mae West* over the top.

'When it came to actually firing your guns at a target once combat had been joined, the Spitfire was also a major improvement over the old Gauntlet, which tended to bob about alarmingly when hit by turbulence thanks to its biplane configuration. Saying that, the Spitfire was not as steady a gun platform as the Hurricane, however. Nevertheless, with its wide gun layout along the wings, the former was ideal for tackling enemy fighters.'

Dunkirk

After eight months of convoy patrols and false interceptions of stray Blenheims and Wellingtons during 'The Phoney War', No 19 Sqn finally entered the conflict proper covering the evacuation of the British Expeditionary Force from Dunkirk in late May 1940. In the brief, but bloody, struggle that took place at the limit of the Spitfire's endurance, George Unwin claimed three kills and two probables.

ABOVE Yet another Channel sweep safely completed, a battle-seasoned Flt Sgt George Unwin climbs out of his Spitfire I K9853 at Fowlmere in late June 1940. To the left of his flying boot is a rare piece of early-war nose art in the form of a *Popeye* figure about to deliver his famous 'Twisker Sock' punch. A member of George's groundcrew had painted this cartoon figure on K9853 several weeks prior to No 19 Sqn going into combat over France in late May. During this period Unwin flew several different Spitfires on combat patrols across the Channel, although this particular machine, coded 'QV-H', was his favourite. Indeed, he claimed a He 111 probable whilst flying K9853 over Dunkirk on his second patrol of 1 June. Earlier that same day he had used K9856 to shoot down a Bf 110 over the evacuation beaches, plus claim a second *Zerstörer* as a probable. 'QV-H' had been with the squadron since 31 January 1939, first being flown by Unwin on 15 March that same year. After serving with the unit for almost 18 months, it was sent to General Aircraft Limited for overhaul on 15 July 1940 following No 19 Sqn's re-equipment with the less than successful cannon-armed Mk IB. K9853 was issued to Training Command the following month, and was written off in a heavy landing before the end of September *(George Unwin)*

'We had been keyed up and raring to go throughout "The Phoney War", and fellows like Harry Steere and myself, with four years of experience already behind us, felt totally confident in our ability to meet any challenge, particularly with the Spitfire as our mount. Despite feeling confident of my chances once combat was joined, I still remember that I froze solid in my cockpit when the first Bf 109 attacked me. I could see this aircraft (a Bf 109E-3 of I./JG 51) diving down in an arc towards me, with what looked like sparks lighting up his wings – I then realised that he was shooting at me, and all I could do was sit there in the cockpit and watch him, I was so fascinated! I was shaken from my stupor when two shells hit my aircraft behind the cockpit, and took evasive action. Fortunately I survived this brief moment of "stage fright" and never hesitated again – many pilots new to combat had similar experiences, but never lived to tell the tale.

'My first victory was scored on 27 May, the day after I "froze", and it consisted of a cheeky Henschel Hs 126 spotter aircraft (of 4.(H)/22, Ed.). The little bugger had used his superior manoeuvrability and slow speed to evade a series of attacks by Flt Lt "Sandy" Lane and Flg Off Frank Brinsden whilst I held off looking for enemy fighters. All the while he was rapidly retreating into occupied Belgium, and Lane finally gave up and ordered us to return to base. Just as they turned their back on him he straightened out to fly away and, feigning R/T failure, I dived on him out of the sun – he saw me too late, and despite

RIGHT The legendary Douglas Bader (left) served very briefly with George Unwin at No 19 Sqn in the spring of 1940. During this time the future Duxford Wing leader destroyed Spitfire I K9858 whilst trying to take-off in coarse pitch. He is seen here in 1945 at Duxford with Sqn Ldr Alexander Hess, who served with No 310 'Czech' Sqn as part of Bader's 'Big Wing' during the Battle of Britain *(via Bruce Robertson)*

an attempted stall and spiral dive, I pumped 240 rounds into the aircraft and it caught fire and crashed.

'The weird thing about shooting down aircraft was that you never thought about actually hurting the occupant – rather, I concentrated on destroying the *aeroplane*. The horror of war only really struck home following a harrowing experience endured by my good friend Harry Steere when he and I each downed a Bf 109E over Dunkirk on the same mission, 24 hours after my Henschel victory. The Messerschmitt fighter had an L-shaped fuel tank precariously positioned immediately behind and below the cockpit seat, and once hit it soon burst into flames. The pilot of Steere's machine got halfway out the cockpit before the flames engulfed him, all in sight of poor Harry.'

Flt Sgt Steere was so shook up that he was physically ill during the return flight to Hornchurch.

Following Dunkirk No 19 Sqn returned to the mundane routine of convoy patrols, although a new task in the form of night interception of lone nuisance raiders was also thrust upon the unit, with limited success. In late June the squadron began to re-equip with the first cannon-armed Mk IBs, and although George and his fellow pilots were initially honoured to have been chosen as the first unit to receive the type, this elation soon evaporated.

'When we got hold of the first brand new cannon-Spitfires we were more than a little peturbed by the fact that we had only six seconds worth of ammunition to shoot – little did we know that stoppages would restrict us ever using all 60 rounds carried for each gun! To this day, no one has ever given me a suitable explanation as to how these 30 Mk IBs with the initial cannon fit ever passed pre-service gunnery test.'

As soon as the wing experienced a modicum of 'g', it twisted slightly due to aerolasticity and the tightly fitting ammunition drum inside the elliptical structure would rub against the wing skinning and quickly jam, trapping the rounds inside. The ejection of spent cartridges was also a major problem due to the weapons' installation, engineers having fitted the gun on its side because of the thinness of the Spitfire wing.

'By laying the 20 mm weapon on its side the belt feed tension was slackened, resulting in the nose of the shell moving around as soon as "g" was pulled on, and jamming in the breech. Once this occurred you couldn't clear the blockage in the air, and once one cannon stopped it was like trying to fly a twin-engined aeroplane on one engine due to the pull exerted on the fighter from the other gun when it fired!'

George had to fight this vicious swing when he claimed a Bf 110C of 2./ZG 26 during an evening interception of 50 Messerschmitt 'twins' performed by A Flight of No 19 Sqn on 16 August 1940. This was the first serious action the unit had seen since Dunkirk, and marked the less than happy debut of the cannon-armed Mk IB. Three Bf 110s were claimed destroyed, two from ZG 26 and one from ZG 76, although German losses revealed that one of these machine limped home with 80 per cent damage sustained – this was a Stab./ZG 26 machine claimed by George as a probable. In return a Spitfire flown by Sgt Henry Roden received Cat 1 damage.

Combat Report

The Form 'F' filled out by Flt Sgt Unwin straight after landing back at Coltishall reported the action in the following terms:

'I was Red 3 with Flt Lt Lane and Sgt Roden. We left Coltishall at 1715 and were ordered to vector at 15,000 ft (which was later changed to 12,000 ft). After vectoring for about 20 minutes a large formation of E/A (100 approximately) were sighted ahead and slightly above. They were escorted by a large number of Me 110s behind, which were searching. Above was an escort of Me 109s. We tried to reach the bombers unobserved but were sighted by the rear 110's (about 30). We immediately engaged and I gave a 110 (of Stab./ZG 26, Ed.) a short burst at close range, and he half rolled and went vertically down. I was immediately attacked by another 110 but managed to get rid of him. On turning, I found myself presented with a perfect target. I fired all my rounds into him and he fell over on his side with bits falling off. He dived steeply and his tail came off. I followed him down and on coming through the clouds I saw the end of a splash. I returned to base at 1830 hours.'

Further additional information on the sortie gleaned by the squadron Intelligence Officer went as follows;

'My starboard cannon had a stoppage.

'Bombers were in a vic of five. Fighters in a vic of five, except the 110s at rear, which were searching. Normal camouflage and markings. Blue underside.

'Fighter Command attack – not in book.

'No rear fire, but at least four machine guns firing forward and some cannon fire at times. E/A firing from fixed forward guns only. E/A fired at long range and inaccurate, therefore no effect.

'During attack E/A only used turning as evasive tactics, and did not use the system of fighting in pairs. After attack E/A crashed in sea.

'Weather - 9/10ths cloud 4000 to 7000 ft.

'Attack was carried out from the sun.

'Speed of formation 180 mph.

'Course - 150°.'

When interviewed for this book some 55 years after (almost to the day) the aforementioned sortie off the coast of Harwich, George added the following thoughts on his victory – the first of literally thousands by cannon-armed Spitfires in RAF service;

'I only had one gun operating following my first burst at the Bf 110 formation. In order to have any chance of scoring hits with the remaining gun, I had to kick on full opposite rudder to offset the recoil when it fired – this didn't help your accuracy at all. I quickly learnt that the only way to secure hits was to get right up the enemy's backside and give him a good burst, which wasn't that long with a Mk IB! I got so close to this aircraft that I nearly cut his twin fins off with my propeller.'

Appropriately, No 19 Sqn's last kill with the Mk IB also fell to George Unwin, and this again was a Bf 110C-2 from ZG 26, but this time from the 7th *Staffel*. His combat report for 3 September reads;

'I was on patrol leading Red Section in the Squadron. We were at 20,000 ft over base (Duxford or Debden, Ed.). Towards the South we saw smoke and AA bursts. On investigating we saw approximately 50 bombers in tight formation flying East. We formed line astern and climbed into the sun in front of the bombers intending to take on the fighters. My CO turned to attack and then I saw a Me 110 turn towards him. This machine was about a mile in front of the other enemy aircraft, apparently a look out. On sighting me he turned away and I gave a very short deflection burst but missed. However, he then flew straight and I closed to 100 yards and blew his port engine out. He still flew, so as there was no return fire I closed right in and gave him the rest of my port gun, as my starboard had stopped. His starboard engine fell out and the pilot baled out. Aircraft crashed South of Malden, I think near Battlesbridge. In any case, he crashed at the inland point of one of the rivers.

'Markings camouflage normal.

'Enemy fighters seemed to be flying in no fixed

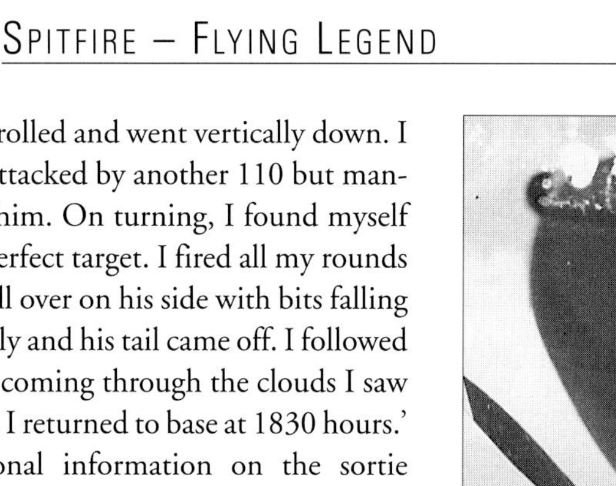

ABOVE 'QV-I', alias X4474, has its guns hurriedly tended at Fowlmere in late September 1940, in anticipation of its next scramble. Already strapped into the cockpit, Sgt Bernard Jennings chats with his rigger about some rectification work carried out on X4474 since his last flight in the machine

RIGHT Jennings and X4474 didn't have to sit around for long, as Yellow Section, led by George Unwin, soon got the word to scramble from Fowlmere. On Friday, 27 September 1940, this combat pairing were credited with the destruction of a Bf 109E from JG 54, downed during a huge dogfight south of the Thames that saw No 19 Sqn pilots claim a further seven *Emils* destroyed

formation, but in a bunch at varying heights. Weather fine and cloudless.

'Landed 1115. Rounds fired – 6 in starboard, 60 in port.'

Two other ZG 26 machines were claimed by No 19 Sqn during this sortie, the last to be flown by the unit in the near-useless Mk IB. Later that same day, following a direct order from No 12 Group Commander-in-Chief, Air Vice-Marshal Trafford Leigh-Mallory, the squadron exchanged its near-new Spitfires for a dozen 'clapped out' ex-OTU Mk IAs – 'and what wrecks, but at least their guns fire', was the verdict in the squadron's daily record book.

Fortunately for George, his 'new' machine (P9546/'QV-H') had come from a maintenance unit at Hendon, following its brief service at the station with No 257 Sqn. This unit had worked up with Spitfires, but then had them inexplicably taken away and replaced with Hurricanes in June, with the result that P9546 had remained unused at the airfield ever since. It wasn't to remain that way for long – George used it to claim a pair of Bf 109Es destroyed on 7 September, followed four days later by a He 111. His engine and windscreen were hit later in the same sortie when he tackled a lone Do 17 over North Weald;

'At about 1600 on 11 September, I was flying P9546 as Red 4 with Sqn Ldr B J E Lane when we intercepted a large number of enemy aircraft over east London. I attacked a Do 215 (Do 17, Ed.) at about 15,000 ft from astern. I concentrated on the rear gunner in the "dustbin" below the fuselage and opened fire at about 350 yards. He returned fire but ceased after I had delivered a couple of bursts. Assuming I had put the gunner out of action, I closed in from below and opened fire at a range of about 200 yards. I carried on firing whilst closing in until suddenly the gunner opened up again – whether this was the same chap who had been shooting at me before I will never know. Suddenly a hole appeared in the armoured part of the windscreen (we later found the armour-piercing round on the cockpit floor) and I was enveloped in smoke. I immediately thought that I was dead!

'I broke off the attack by diving away to port. Thinking I was on fire I switched off the ignition and petrol, undid my straps and opened the canopy with the intention of bailing out. I then saw that the smoke was coming from the front of the engine and realised that it must be burning glycol, which I could also smell, from a damaged cooling pipe atop the engine. I strapped myself back into the cockpit and began to look for a suitable place to land. I spotted quite a large grass field occupied by cattle near Brentwood, in Essex. I carried out a wheels down forced landing with no damage to the aircraft, and almost immediately a jeep arrived, and a young subaltern and two soldiers with fixed bayonets greeted me as I stepped out the cockpit.

'With their assistance I took the top cowling off and checked the shattered cooling pipe. North Weald was only eight miles away, so leaving one soldier guarding the Spitfire, we drove off to the badly bombed-out fighter station. I knew many of the NCO pilots based here with Nos 56 and 151 Sqns, and with their help I arranged for a fitter to repair my machine the following day.

'North Weald was a real mess, and following a solid drinking session with my ex-No 19 Sqn mate, Flt Sgt "Taffy" Higginson, I was put to bed in a damaged hut near one of the dispersals. Ack-ack fire during the night was incessant, but I slept very well due no doubt to the volume of alcohol consumed! I returned to Fowlmere with a temporarily patched up P9546 the next day, having been posted missing for 24 hours – there were no operable phones at North Weald to inform No 19 Sqn of my whereabouts. As for the Dornier, I never knew what happened to it. However, it certainly could not have been in mint condition as I had fired almost all my ammunition into it at quite close range.'

Triple kill

September 15 is today celebrated as Battle of Britain Day, and fittingly, is was on this climactic Sunday back in 1940 that George Unwin enjoyed his best 24 hours in combat. His first victory of the day was a Bf 109E-4 flown by 3./JG 53 *Staffelkapitan* Oblt Julius Haase, shot down near Biggin Hill during the Duxford Wing's morning patrol over south London. The official combat report stated;

'I was Red Three with Flt Lt Lawson. We sighted the E/A who were in vics of three. The escorts dived singly on us, and I engaged one of them (Me 109) with a yellow nose. I gave one burst of six seconds and E/A burst into flames. Pilot baled out. I searched around for half-an-hour but could not find any other E/A. I landed at 1250.'

After returning to Fowlmere and filling in their respective Form 'F's, the pilots had hardly had time to catch breath when word came through of eight to ten large enemy formations massing over the Channel. Scrambled late from their airfields in No 12 Group, the five-squadron strong Duxford Wing struggled to formate and gain height before tackling the Luftwaffe over London. George Unwin takes up the story;

'I was lucky to survive that second sortie unscathed, as through my own stupidity I got separated from the rest of the Wing. We were led through a gap in the cloud over London by Sqn Ldr Douglas Bader of No 242 Sqn, and there in front of us was a sight that looked just like a pre-war Hendon Air Pageant flypast. We were at about 23,000 ft and the bombers were below us at 20,000. I was transfixed by a squadron of Hurricanes struggling to engage these aircraft, and I had completely forgotten about their escort – I flew straight into the middle of them! The next thing I knew literally thousands of yellow-nosed Messerschmitts were whistling by all around me less than 100 yards away, so I pulled the bloody stick back, went into a steep turn, and held it there!

'I gave the odd machine a quick burst as it flew past me, and succeeded in forcing one to half roll and dive into cloud below. I followed him down, but my windscreen froze at 6000 ft and he escaped. I then climbed back up to 25,000 ft in search of my wingmates, but as was often the case in these aerial duels, the sky had gone from being heavy with aircraft to totally empty in a matter of seconds. After several minutes I spotted a pair of Bf 109s above me flying back in a loose "rotte" formation towards the Channel, obviously intent on heading home. After a long chase, I finally caught them as they crossed the Kent coast at Lydd, and after firing a long burst into the trailing fighter it immediately burst into flames and crashed just offshore. Inexplicably, the leader failed to take any evasive action and he too was shot down on fire into the sea seconds later.

'I had survived this mission simply because the Spitfire could sustain a continuous rate of turn inside the Bf 109E without stalling – the latter was known for flicking into a vicious stall spin without prior warning if pulled around too tightly. The Spitfire would give a shudder to signal that it was close to the edge, so as soon as you felt the shake you eased off the stick pressure.'

The Mk II

By late September No 19 Sqn had replaced its Mk IAs with the improved Mk II, which boasted a constant-speed Rotol propeller and an uprated Merlin XII powerplant. This aircraft was instantly popular with George Unwin, who by now was a seasoned combat veteran with 11 kills to his credit, and a DFM to match.

Such was his knowledge of the enemy, and their tactics, he regularly led the last vic of three – the Search, or 'arse-end Charlie', slot as he describes it 55 years later. With his superb eyesight, Unwin was a natural for this position, and often spotted the Luftwaffe fighters diving down on the Duxford Wing before his squadron-mates.

'We were always on the defensive due to their greater ceiling, and our staple tactic was to turn straight into them so that they couldn't latch onto your tail. You then pulled on the "g" in the hope that your own superior rate of turn would allow you to whip around on to their tails. Often, having performed this manoeuvre on two or three consecutive occasions, you would right yourself only to find the sky empty of friend or foe! Then the search began all over again.'

George Unwin survived the Battle of Britain and was finally promoted to Warrant Officer and sent to Cranwell to learn to be an instructor in December 1940. Having been initially deemed both war-weary and too old for frontline flying, George proved the latter judgement to be wide of the mark by returning to ops with No 613 Sqn in 1944 on intruder missions over Europe in Mosquito Mk VIs. Thus ended his five-year spell with No 19 Sqn. As a farewell 'gift' from his CO, George and his good friend Harry Steere teamed up with Sqn Ldr Lane to perform formation aerobatics over Duxford in true pre-war fashion. This was George's very last flight in a No 19 Sqn Spitfire.

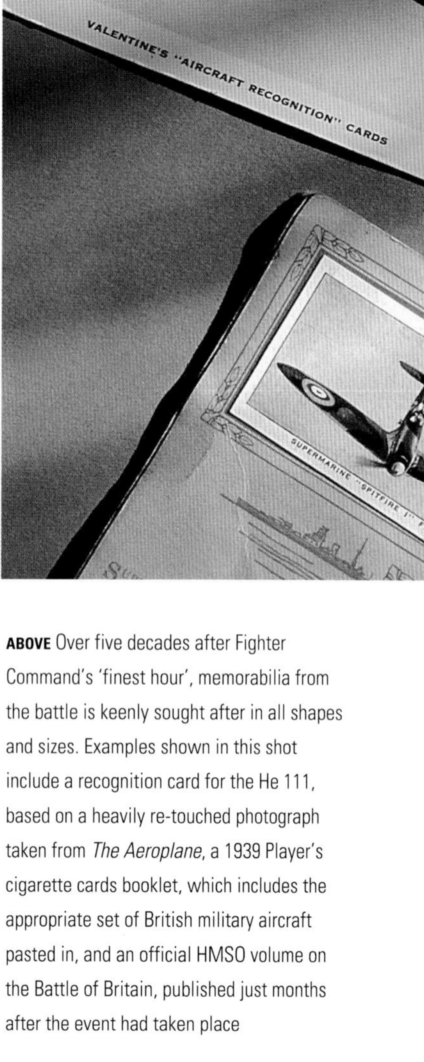

ABOVE Over five decades after Fighter Command's 'finest hour', memorabilia from the battle is keenly sought after in all shapes and sizes. Examples shown in this shot include a recognition card for the He 111, based on a heavily re-touched photograph taken from *The Aeroplane*, a 1939 Player's cigarette cards booklet, which includes the appropriate set of British military aircraft pasted in, and an official HMSO volume on the Battle of Britain, published just months after the event had taken place

RIGHT An original FORM "F" Combat Report is a highly-prized 'artefact' for students of the battle. This document belongs to George Unwin, and details a highly eventful sortie flown by him in Spitfire I P9546 on the afternoon of 11 September 1940. Unwin was officially commended by his superiors at Fighter Command HQ following his forced landing of the 'engineless' Spitfire mentioned in this report

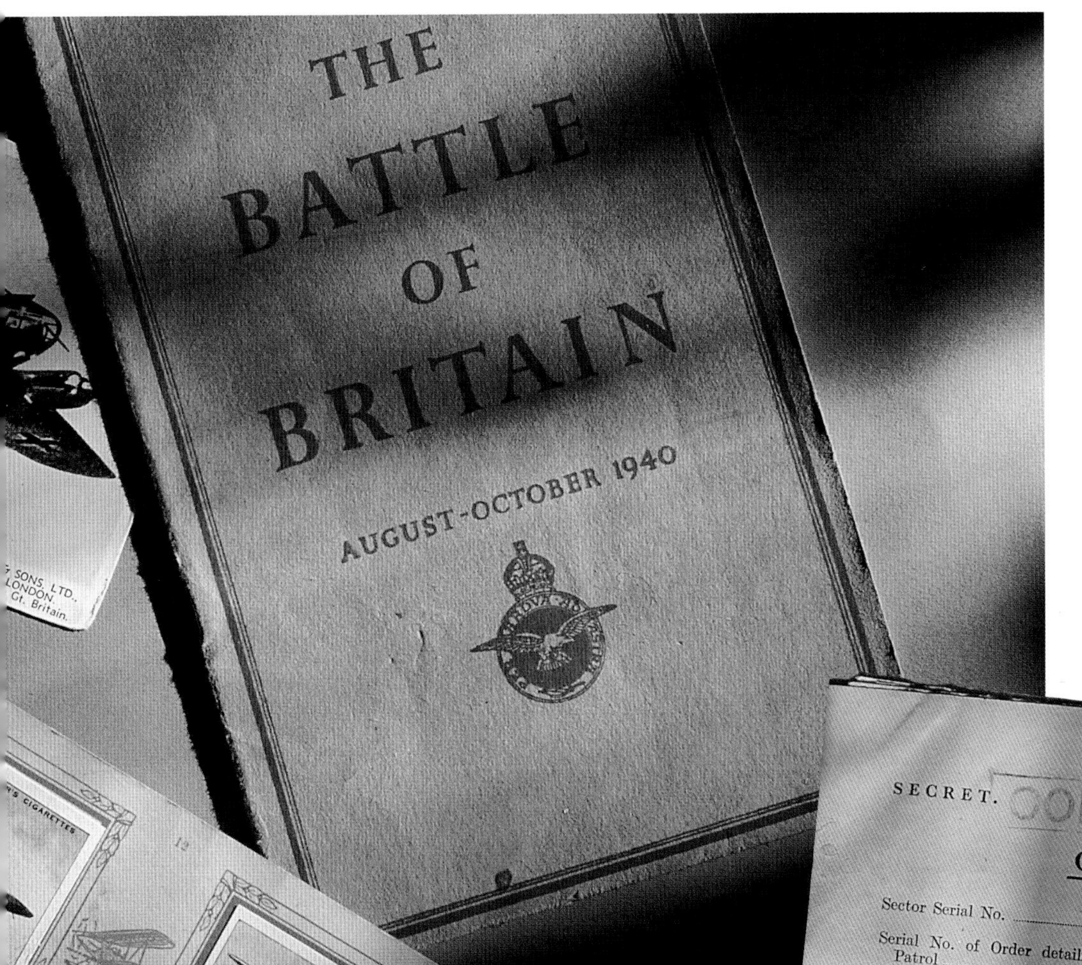

He finally left the RAF in 1961 with the rank of Wing Commander, possessing a veritable armful of log books filled with flying hours on myriad front-line types.

Like many of his contemporaries, George was attracted back to the Spitfire in 1968 when he was invited to Duxford by 'Ginger' Lacey to witness the making of the film *The Battle of Britain*. It was here, all those years after he had flown off into combat from the Cambridgeshire airfield, that he found that his affection for the Mk II was shared by a new generation of RAF fighter pilots. He explained;

'There is no doubt about the fact that the Mk II was *the* flying machine when it came to the Spitfire. The Mk IX was clearly a better fighter, certainly when it came to Merlin-powered Spitfires, but it wasn't a flying machine like the Mk II, which enjoyed the best balance of power to weight. This was proven to me conclusively at Duxford in 1968. Whilst I was there I had lunch with the serving RAF pilots who were flying the Spitfires for the film, and I remarked that I had seen a Mk II (P7350) amongst the machines lined up on the field.

'Several of them immediately replied that it was a real fight to get to fly this machine, as opposed to the other Mk Vs, IXs and XIVs involved in the filming. Upon enquiring as to why this was the case, they simply replied that it was different from the rest – somehow smoother, although none of them could quite define why. The Mk II really was a beautiful machine. You only had to lean or breathe on the control column and it instantly responded, as opposed to pulling a machine around like I had to do with some of the later types of aircraft I flew.'

Despite his many commands during three decades of RAF service across the globe, George Unwin always looks back on his two-and-a-half years on Spitfires with No 19 Sqn at Duxford as the pinnacle of his career as a fighter pilot.

SECRET. COPY

Pilot's individual
COMBAT REPORT.

Sector Serial No. .... (A)
Serial No. of Order detailing Flight or Squadron to Patrol .... (B) 34
Date .... (C) 11/9/40
Flight, Squadron .... (D) Flight: A Sqdn.
Number of Enemy Aircraft .... (E) 100 approx.
Type of Enemy Aircraft .... (F) Me.109 Me.110 He.111 Do.215
Time Attack was delivered .... (G) 1600 hours approx.
Place Attack was delivered .... (H) Over East London.
Height of Enemy .... (J) 15000 feet.
Enemy Casualties .... (K) 1 probable. 1 damaged.
Our Casualties Aircraft .... (L) One U/S.
Personnel .... (M) Nil.
GENERAL REPORT .... (R) I was Red 4 with S/Ldr.
Lane. I sighted a large enemy formation on our starboard and below.
We attacked in line astern, forming echelon port. I attacked a He.111
and fired a 7 or 8 second burst at 50 yards range. Bits came off
both engines and the E/A went into a steep spiral. I did not see the
crash, as I was immediately attacked by a Do. 215. I opened fire from
below at 100 yards, closing to 50 yards. I fired all my rounds into
him, but did not see any result, owing to the fact that my windscreen
and engine were shot up by the fire from the bottom gunner. My engine
was running badly as I dived away and was pouring out smoke, which was,
in my opinion, glycol. I switched off and force-landed with my wheels
down. No damage was done to the aircraft on landing. Place of landing
1 mile north of Brentwood near Searchlight Site E.C.11.

Signature G.C. UNWIN F/Sgt.
O.C. Section Red
Flight A
Squadron 19 Squadron No.

(1611) Wt. 33246—

ABOVE In 1996, six decades after K5054's first flight, only a single Spitfire I still regularly graces the skies over Britain – Victor Gauntlett's Mk IA AR213. The narrowness of the cockpit is clearly apparent from this view, and is one of the first features of the design to strike a novice Spitfire pilot. In the summer of 1940, a broad-shouldered young Pilot Officer by the name of James Edgar Johnson was struggling to come to terms with the 'oppressive' confines of the Spitfire at No 7 OTU. He complained to his instructor that his forearms constantly rubbed on the cockpit sides when he sat strapped in on his parachute pack, but fortunately he persevered with the fighter. By VE-Day, the now Wg Cdr 'Johnnie' Johnson had claimed 38 kills in the Spitfire, making him Fighter Command's leading ace on the Channel front

RIGHT AR213 has for many years been regularly flown and maintained by famed aerobatic pilot Tony Bianchi, who is seen here at the controls over a cloudy Oxfordshire on 19 October 1995

LEFT AND BELOW
Built at the Westland Aircraft works at Yeovil a full year after the Battle of Britain had been fought, AR213 was one of the last Mk IAs constructed. Considered to be outclassed by the Mk VB for Channel front ops, it was delivered to the storage depot of No 12 MU at Kirkbride on 24 July 1941. AR213 was sent to No 57 OTU at Hawarden a week later, where it somehow survived the heavy-handed rigours of life in Flying Training Command until suffering a Cat Ac accident on 19 April 1943 whilst with No 53 OTU at Llandow. Repairs were affected quickly, and it had returned to the OTU by 12 May

ABOVE AND RIGHT Sadly, AR213 was to once more suffer at the hands of an over-zealous Pilot Officer less than six months later, although it was back from the repair unit by 10 December. Its was finally retired from No 57 OTU on 17 August 1944, having never fired a shot in anger. AR213 remained in storage with No 8 MU at Little Rissington for the next three years, just one of thousands of redundant Spitfires left to rot at airfields across the UK. Having been struck of charge on 30 November 1945, it awaited the scrapper's torch – quite how its survived until 1947 remains something of a mystery. Finally, in March of that year it was bought for the rumoured sum of £25.00 by RAE Farnborough's Experimental Flying Department boss, Grp Capt Allen Wheeler, following a brief external inspection

LEFT Far from being a classic aircraft 'buff', Wheeler had his sights firmly fixed on entering a Spitfire in the lucrative sponsored air races, scheduled to re-commence in 1948 after a wartime lull of almost a decade. Air racing was responsible for the survival of a number of wartime fighters both in the UK and, on a much larger scale, 'across the pond' in America. Registered G-AIST, AR213 was never destined to wing its way around the pylons, however, being sent by road instead to Old Warden, where Wheeler stuck it in a shed and forgot about it. In the meantime, his search for a more powerful racing mount had led him to acquire Mk VB AB910, which was indeed rebuilt for competition. Whilst the Mk VB embarked on a racing career, AR213 collected dust, eventually following its owner, having now risen to the rank of Air Commodore, to Abingdon, where it sat until 1967.

Flying AR213 on this sortie, performed on 19 October 1995, is Carolyn Grace of ML407 fame. This was her first ever flight in a single-seat Spitfire

LEFT AND ABOVE
In 1967 AR213 was one of many 'warbirds' surveyed by Grp Capt Hamish Mahaddie for possible employment in the film *The Battle of Britain*, which was to be shot in the UK the following year. Thanks to firm backing from United Artists, AR213 was one of three early mark Spitfires chosen for restoration to airworthiness, and the machine was duly transported to RAF Henlow, where the rebuild took place – work was carried out by Simpson's Aeroservices of Elstree

RIGHT AND INSET Aside from the replacement of the centre spar (which came from Mk XVI TB863 – see chapter 7), the aircraft needed only cosmetic rectification to achieve airworthiness. Following its co-starring role in the film, AR213 was transferred by Allen Wheeler from Duxford to Booker, were he flew it for several years in its original No 53 OTU scheme, with appropriate 'QG-A' codes. Wheeler sold the Spitfire to The Honourable Patrick Lindsay in 1971, who placed it in the care of Personal Plane Services (PPS), again at Booker. It was here that PPS manager, and former British aerobatic team member, Tony Bianchi, became involved with the aircraft, and the two have remained inseparable ever since. Patrick Lindsay sadly died in 1986 from cancer, and after a period of speculation as to the fate of AR213, it was jointly bought by ex-Aston Martin director, Victor Gauntlett, and businessman Peter Livanos, who have kept it with PPS.

In the large photo, the aircraft is seen taxying in at Booker on 19 October 1995. The steam venting from the overflow pipe below the exhaust stubs denotes nothing more serious than the Merlin engine's ethylene glycol coolant having reached boiling point at around 130°C during the flight – a common occurrence with the single-radiator Mk Is, IIs and Vs. Vickers-Supermarine test pilot Jeffrey Quill experienced problems with this vent at 25,000 ft whilst flying Spitfire Is with No 65 Sqn during the height of the Battle of Britain. A combination of full power and low airspeeds would rapidly bring the coolant to the boil, and the escaping steam had a habit of freezing all over the windscreen as it was carried back by the airflow
(Tony Holmes)

FAR INSET For many years AR213 has worn the 'PR' codes of No 609 Sqn, but PPS are hoping to soon repaint the fighter in the lurid red and white striped 'bounce aircraft' scheme it briefly wore with No 57 OTU in the winter of 1941 – this rare shot shows evidence of the unusual nose decoration. During its time with the OTU it was often flown by the renowned Flg Off 'Ginger' Lacey, one of the RAF's leading aces
(Peter R Arnold)

JZ E
213

PM M2
PA474
YT F
P7350

LEFT Another Spitfire made airworthy thanks to *The Battle of Britain* film was Mk IIA P7350, seen here escorting the BBMF's Lancaster B 1(FE) PA474 over Lincolnshire farmland in 1992 – Sqn Ldr Al Martin is at the controls of the Spitfire on this occasion. The oldest flyable Supermarine fighter in the world, this machine was the 14th of 11,939 Spitfires built at Castle Bromwich, leaving the huge 'shadow factory' in early August 1940. After passing through No 6 MU at Brize Norton, it was issued as to No 266 'Rhodesia' Sqn at Wittering on 6 September – this battle-weary unit had been pulled back to No 12 Group to re-equip with Mk IIAs. After a short conversion period, No 266 Sqn was flung back into action once again from Hornchurch, taking P7350 with it

BELOW P7350 has worn a number of different schemes over the years as a mark of respect to the pilots who flew with Fighter Command. At the beginning of the 1990s it was the turn of No 65 'East India' Sqn to be honoured, an appropriate summer 1941 scheme being chosen. In this atmospheric shot, taken in July of that year, the unit can be seen taxying out of their dispersals at Kirton-in-Lindsey at the start of a squadron-strength North Sea convoy patrol on a gloomy summer's morning. As can be seen from the four (and a bit!) Mk IIAs visible in this shot, the markings applied to P7350 are totally authentic, although none boast quite as glossy a finish as the pristine BBMF machine

S

LEFT 'Don't fire until you see the whites of their eyes!' – no doubt Flt Lt Paul Shenton had a good view of John Dibbs' 'baby blues' as the latter sat in the Lancaster's tail turret taking this 'up close and personal' view in 1994. Turning the clock back 54 years, P7350 had participated in numerous 'Rhodesia' Squadron patrols in September and early October 1940, before being passed onto fellow Hornchurch-based unit No 603 'City of Edinburgh' Sqn, who commenced operations with Mk IIA Spitfires mid-month. After a brief two week stay, it suffered a Cat B accident on 31 October and was sent to the legendary No 1 Civil Repair Unit at Cowley for rebuilding. By 15 November it had been returned to airworthiness, but its immediate future was spent in storage at No 37 MU at Burtonwood, in Lancashire. Its frontline career recommenced on 18 March 1941 when it was sent to Tangmere for use by No 616 'County of South Yorkshire' Sqn, who were then flying Channel sweeps as part of the Bader Wing

LEFT AND ABOVE Less than a month later P7350 made a return to Hornchurch, where it was flown by No 64 Sqn until August. By the late summer of 1941, the aircraft was in desperate need of an overhaul, so it was duly sent to Scottish Aviation Ltd at Prestwick for a five-and-a-half-month rework. When it emerged in late January 1942, the Mk II's days as a frontline fighter were all but over, so P7350 was relegated to training tasks. During the next two-and-a-half years it spent time with the Central Gunnery School and No 57 OTU, suffering Cat B accidents with both units. P7350 was finally 'pensioned off' to No 39 MU at Colerne on 24 July 1944, where it sat until sold for scrap to John Dale & Sons Ltd in 1947. The idea of an ironmonger with a sense of history when it comes to old aircraft may seem unbelievable, but fortunately someone in the company took one look at its log books and donated the fighter back to the RAF Colerne museum. As with AR213, the making of the *Battle of Britain* saw P7350 returned to airworthiness by John 'Tubby' Simpson, and once shooting had been completed, it was given to the BBMF, where it has stayed ever since

CHAPTER TWO

SHUTTLEWORTH SPITFIRE

Spitfire LF Mk VC AR501

Squadron Leader Pete Brothers
Nos 457 (RAAF) and 602 Sqns, and Tangmere Wing Leader
June 1941 to July 1943

'It quickly became obvious to us in No 11 Group flying sweeps over France that the Fw 190 was clearly superior to our Mk Vs right from the start. Morale was affected to a certain extent, but we felt that on the whole we were better pilots than the Germans, and could just about cope with this new threat. We still had confidence in the soundness of our Spitfires, and we simply treated the Focke-Wulf with more respect than a Bf 109F. On the whole, the Fw 190 was far less prevalent in combat in 1941 than the Messerschmitt. However, by the time my Australian squadron (No 457) had moved down to the "front-line" at No 11 Group in March 1942, after spending

ABOVE By the late summer of 1941 No 72 Sqn had moved to Biggin's satellite field at Gravesend, which had briefly served as home for the unit in June 1940. Despite relocation, the squadron kept up its hectic tasking of near daily wing sweeps over France. It was now more than proficient with the cannon-armed Mk VB, the first of which had been issued to No 72 Sqn in place of their Mk IIBs upon their arrival at Biggin in July. Perhaps the most famous action in which the unit was involved during World War 2 occurred not long after this dispersal 'beat-up' shot was taken. It saw No 72 Sqn Spitfires attempting to escort the ill-fated Swordfish strike on the German battlecruisers *Scharnhorst* and *Gneisenau* during the 'Channel Dash' of 12 February 1942

LEFT During the summer of 1941 No 72 Sqn, led by veteran Australian Battle of Britain ace Sqn Ldr Des Sheen, formed an integral part of the Biggin Hill Wing. In this shot, 'RN-M'/W3316 and 'RN-L'/W3437 (christened *Kaapstad II* following donations from Cape Town residents) of B Flight are readied for a patrol, whilst A Flight's 'RN-P' taxies past prior to take-off

some months on the Isle of Man getting to grips with the Spitfire, the Fw 190 was being regularly encountered over France.

'We were predominantly flying bomber escorts and fighter sweeps in our Mk VBs during 1942/43, participating in sorties with the Kenley, Hornchurch and Biggin Hill Wings – we often flew top cover for the latter outfit. As an example of these missions, one I particularly remember saw us forming part of the rear support wing for 12 Bostons attacking the Hazebrouck marshalling yards in France. To fill this crucial role we would sweep just inland to tackle any German fighters harassing the Circus as it returned to England. Having taken off much later than the main formation, we would have far greater reserves of fuel than other fighter escort wings, and it would be up to us to ensure the safe escape of all elements of the Circus.

'Aside from these large formation Circuses, we would also fill our time flying squadron-generated Rodeos along the Channel coast, buzzing known bases on the outskirts of Calais, Wissant and Le Touquet in a big arcing sweep across occupied France. On a more concentrated attack on a single site, we escorted 12 "Hurri-bombers" hitting the airfield at Desvres, south-east of Boulogne – these aircraft were regularly used for ground attack work against power stations too, and we were usually called upon to escort them. As can be seen from most of the names I have mentioned here, our Circus and Rodeo sweeps were restricted to targets not too distant from the Channel, due to the limited legs of the Mk V Spitfire – one hour and fifteen-minute sorties were the norm for 1941-42, although I did crack one hour and thirty minutes on several occasions, and came home very "dry". The furthest inland we would dare go on an escort mission was Paris, and even then you had to manage the Merlin just right to ensure a frugal fuel intake – weak mixture, power set to cruise, full throttle to achieve low revs and coarse pitch on the propeller.

'Because of our limited radius of action, if we were jumped we couldn't usually rush off after our opponents if they flew a diving attack through the bombers from their usual position several thousand feet above us. However, if they stuck around to press home an attack, or we spotted them first, you immediately changed the prop pitch to fine and built up speed to enter the fray – having the throttle already at maximum revs helped us build up to combat speed quite quickly, and the clever pilot always kept one eye on the enemy and the other on the fuel gauge. Despite these combat restrictions, they didn't prevent me from claiming a Fw 190 probable on 29 April 1942 over Griz Nez whilst I led No 457 Sqn as part of the diversion wing – this was a great dogfight, with the enemy putting up a large formation of fighters to oppose us.'

No 602 Sqn

Having overseen the establishment of the second 'Australian' fighter unit formed in the UK, and schooled its pilots as they progressed from flying patrols over the Irish Sea in war-weary Spitfire Mk Is and IIs to combat patrols over France in Mk VBs, Pete Brothers remained at Redhill to take command of veteran Fighter Command outfit No 602 Sqn 'City of Glasgow'. No 457, meanwhile, relocated to Darwin, Australia, as part of the wing despatched to protect the nation from Japanese attack.

Pete Brothers' new command had been part of the scene at Redhill and Kenley since July 1941, the auxiliary squadron receiving brand new Mk VBs in place of their Mk IIAs upon their arrival at the Surrey fighter station. Over the ensuing year the unit had flown a countless number of Circuses, often performing two or three ops in a single day. Like most other No 11 Group units of this period, No 602 Sqn had suffered steady losses at the hands of both Bf 109 and Fw 190 *Gruppe* during their time on the Channel front, and when Pete Brothers arrived to relieve the recently-promoted Wg Cdr 'Paddy' Finucane, he found a collection of war-weary pilots ready for a rest. Morale suffered a further setback just days after Brothers' arrival when Finucane was killed on one of his first sweeps with the Hornchurch Wing, where he had recently assumed command – two days later, on 17 July 1942, No 602 Sqn was posted north out of the frontline.

At that time air stations in Nos 13 and 14 Groups were seen as the place for a tired unit to recharge and regroup, so remote Peterhead, north of Aberdeen, was chosen as home for No 602 Sqn. An influx of new pilots had to be moulded into frontline material, and Pete Brothers was just the man for the job, having served with Nos 32 and 257 Sqns as a flight commander during both the Battles of France and Britain two years before. He had also seen much offensive service with No 457 Sqn in the first half of 1942. Four to six months away from the fighting was the usual rest period for a squadron in Fighter Command, so it came as something of a surprise to Sqn Ldr Brothers when he was informed that his unit was being posted back to Biggin Hill on 16 August, barely four weeks after arriving in Peterhead. A special assignment awaited them – supporting Operation *Jubilee*, better known simply as the Dieppe raid.

In order to temporarily wrest air superiority from the Luftwaffe over the beach-head for the 19 August assault, the AOC of No 11 Group, Air Vice-Marshal Trafford Leigh-Mallory, requested the allocation of no less than 48 Spitfire squadrons to his command. One of those assigned on a temporary basis was No 602 Sqn, who journeyed back down south to Biggin Hill three days prior to the raid. Despite only staying 'on the bump' for three days, the unit definitely made its presence felt over France, as Pete Brothers recounted for this volume;

'We saw plenty of action during the days leading up to the actual landings, and in order to expose many of our new guys to fighter sweeps prior to the big day, I accepted an invitation from fellow Biggin-based No 222 Sqn (led by veteran Battle of Britain ace 'Bobby' Oxspring, Ed.) to join them on a Rodeo along the French coast the day after we arrived. The first sortie was a bit of a mess, with both units departing late, and then having little fuel to fly for any length of time over France. Not surprisingly, we provoked little response from the Luftwaffe, but the following day I planned a sweep solely for No 602 Sqn, which was far more rewarding. We went in east of Dunkirk, then flew around St Omer to try and stir up the incumbents, then departed out over Griz Nez.

BELOW The Mk V was the first truly 'global' Spitfire, being used by the Allies in all major theatres of war. A perfect example of this is provided by 'WR-Z', a weather-beaten Mk VB of No 40 Sqn, South African Air Force (SAAF), seen here parked at the unit's austere dispersal in Tunisia in 1943. In order to make the Merlin engine reliable when subjected to the both the heat and the fine desert dust of North Africa, Mk Vs were initially fitted with an ungainly (and unpopular, due to its performance-sapping attributes) Vokes filtered intake, which was just one of 26 major mods inflicted on the machine to make it more suitable for 'tropical' use. Within weeks of the reworked Spitfires arriving in the Middle East in early 1942, a resourceful team of engineers at No 103 Maintenance Unit at Aboukir had trimmed the fairing down in size, and thus restored the Mk V's 'top end' performance. The Aboukir filter soon became the standard fitment for all Desert Air Force Spitfires, 'WR-Z' included

I claimed a Fw 190 out over enemy shipping moored to the east of Dunkirk, but we lost Flt Sgt Gledhill, who was shot down in flames – fortunately he survived this incident and was made a PoW.

'Operation *Jubilee* itself was interesting in terms of the way it showed how a battle develops. My squadron was one of the first on patrol over the beaches at first light at 2000 ft, and at that point there was virtually no activity at all. We were duly relieved and went back to refuel, and when we returned for our second sweep activity had well and truly started, with the medium bomber formations trying to get up to the cloud base at 4000 ft for protection. As the weather improved we increased our patrolling ceiling to 5000 ft, and by the end of our fourth, and last, sortie in the late afternoon, we were cruising at 20,000 ft! This day perfectly illustrated how crucial the advantage of height is in aerial warfare, and as the weather improved, we took advantage of it accordingly.

'Of the four sweeps we flew that day, the second patrol was the most exciting from our squadron's point of view as we intercepted a large formation of Ju 88s and Do 217s, escorted by a fair number of Fw 190s. I made passes at both types of German bomber, but on every occasion had to break off my attacks due to the overwhelming number of Fw 190s in the area – indeed, my No 2, Plt Off Goodchap, was shot down and captured. Such was the ferocity of the battle, it was impossible to concentrate on downing a single machine, and I had to resort to taking pot shots at enemy aircraft as they passed through my field of fire during my hour-long series of evasive manoeuvres.'

Despite the chaotic nature of the patrol once the enemy had been engaged, No 602 Sqn nevertheless acquitted itself well, claiming three Do 217s destroyed and one probable, and a further six Dorniers damaged, along with a Ju 88 and two Fw 190s – one of the latter pair was claimed by Pete Brothers. The third sweep saw the squadron attempting to prevent enemy dive-bombers attacking British naval vessels supporting the assault. The Spitfires were soon embroiled in bitter dogfights at low-level with a swarm of Fw 190s from JGs 2 and 26, and veteran No 602 Sqn pilot Flt Lt Johnny Niven was shot down and wounded, although he was plucked from the Channel by a Royal Navy corvette and returned to Brighton the same day – no claims were made by the unit in return.

By the end of the day, No 602 Sqn knew they had been involved in an epic action – indeed, the RAF had flown nearly 3000 sorties during the course of the day, and suffered serious losses combating a tenacious enemy. With the raid over, the squadron returned to Scotland the following day, where a signal was awaiting them from No 14 Group AOC, Air Vice-Marshal Raymond Collishaw (one of the leading aces of the Great War), congratulating them on their success over the beach-head.

LEFT Sqn Ldr Pete Brothers had already seen combat over France and south-east England (during which time he had become a double-ace) in Hurricanes by the time he was posted to head the newly-formed No 457 Sqn in June 1941, and found the transition onto the Spitfire relatively straightforward. He was to remain in the frontline with No 11 Group, flying various marks of Spitfire, until VE-Day

Spitfire Mk VI

The monotony of constant patrols over desolate Scotland and northern England was temporarily disrupted for No 602 Sqn in September when a the unit re-equipped with pressurised Spitfire Mk VIs, and deployed to Skaebrae, in the Orkneys, in order to better defend Scapa Flow from high-altitude recce flights. Few were impressed with their new mounts, as Pete Brothers explained;

'With the Mk VI the groundcrew literally screwed you into the cockpit in order to preserve the aircraft's pressurisation. Up at high altitude, the fighter became very stiff on the ailerons and elevators, and once we realised that the Ju 86P flights had all but ceased we took all the pressure seals out, removed the high altitude wing tips, and thus created a clipped-wing Mk VI, which we used to great effect at low-level! We never bothered to return them back to their original configuration, thus leaving these machines in essentially a Mk V fit.'

Brothers was not sad to leave the rare Mk VI behind him when he was posted to Tangmere as wing leader in October 1942, returning to frontline flying in the more conventional Mk VB. Taking over from Wg Cdr 'Johnnie' Walker, he immediately threw himself into leading the Tangmere Wing on virtually daily sweeps over France. Life for a Mk V pilot at this stage in the war was far from easy, as the performance gap between his mount and that of his German opponent had widened dramatically over the course of the year.

'We had our hands full combating the Fw 190 in our Spit Vs, the former possessing virtually unmatched manoeuvrability. Luftwaffe pilots were prepared to mix it with us in the Fw 190 due to its fabulous rate of roll, unlike the Bf 109F/G pilots who tended to rely on sweeping attacks from altitude. The controls in the former fighter were roller bearing, and we saw just how effective this was when Arnim Faber's captured aircraft was demonstrated to us at Tangmere several months after the Dieppe raid. I clearly remember that you could put a penny on the aileron and it would push it down, and its opposite surface on the other wing up, until the coin finally slid off!'

Wing sweep

Although the new Mk IX Spitfire was entering service in increasing numbers, and slowly restoring the balance in favour of Fighter Command, the squadrons in Pete Brothers' wing struggled on with their venerable Mk Vs well into 1943. Despite being hamstrung in performance terms when compared with other No 11 Group wings, the Tangmere boys nevertheless took the fight to the Luftwaffe at every opportunity. One of the units within the wing was No 610 Sqn, at that time commanded by Sqn Ldr 'Johnnie' Johnson, and on 26 January 1943 he and Pete Brothers were involved in an amusing incident, related in the following passages by the latter, after completing a successful sweep over France;

'We had a brand new radar called *Appledore* – after its location in Kent – which could see well into France, and they offered their services to the Hornchurch Wing, who for some inexplicable reason declined their approach, so it was passed on to us. On this particular mission, despite being some miles inland over France, the *Appledore* controllers could still clearly see the Wing, and they told us they were plotting 12 hostiles coming out of Abbeville on their scopes. They gave us both their height and a direction vector for interception, so we swung around and got "up sun" of the enemy, before diving

RIGHT Typical of the action which preceded a wing sweep at airfield dispersals across southern England throughout the war, this anonymous Mk VB has its guns rearmed and fuel topped up prior to the arrival of its pilot. Below the wing are ammunition boxes full of belted .303 in machine gun rounds, ready for insertion into the magazines, whilst to the right of the photo can be seen the cannon shell drum for the 20 mm Hispano

BELOW Just how much the Vokes mod changed the appearance of the Spitfire can be gauged from this shot of a bomb-toting No 2 Sqn, SAAF, Mk VC (note the Springbok emblem on the fin, despite the unit's 'Flying Cheetah' nickname) over Italy in November 1943. Tasked with supporting the 8th Army's push up the Italian 'boot', the squadron made full use of the Spitfire's four-cannon 'C' wing fit in a succession of ground attack sorties which lasted until war's end in May 1945

on them from our superior tactical position. They turned out to be Fw 190s, and as we passed through the formation they broke up, and I took a squirt at one without hitting him.

'We had maintained a reasonable shape as we flew through the enemy and I began to lead the Wing back up again for another pass at them. As I was banking around at about 500 ft I spotted a single Fw 190 diving down at me, so I took him head on at a range of 110 yards in a climbing turn, and the rest of the formation broke around me. Once I had flashed past underneath the diving Focke-Wulf, I looked around for other targets, but could only see a solitary Spitfire which, after forming up with it, I recognised was being flown by "Johnnie" Johnson. We quickly set course for home, having expended our allocated fuel. Our gunnery leader, Flt Lt H R "Dizzy" Allen (a Battle of Britain ace with No 66 Sqn, Ed.), always told us to finish off our ciné gun film with a few frames sighted on an immovable object like a lighthouse, or a formating Spitfire, to ensure that the equipment hadn't shifted during the vibration of firing, and was therefore giving accurate distance readings – victory assessments often hinged on the evidence of the ciné camera.

'With "Dizzy's" instructions firmly in mind, I asked "Johnnie" to move ahead into my sights whilst I shot off the rest of my film. We duly landed back in Sussex without any more drama, and I sent the film off to the assessors for analysis. They confirmed my Fw 190 kill, with plenty of cannon strikes around the cockpit area being seen, followed by the amazing sight of the pilot actually leaving the cockpit! The young chap debriefing me on the contents of the film then went on to say, "The second aircraft that you fired at Wing Commander looks remarkably like a Spitfire!" I quickly informed him that I wasn't firing at it, but just running off my ciné film as per "Dizzy's" instructions. "Oh yes, of course, sir", was his sheepish reply, but to this day I don't think he believed me – rather that I shot at the Spitfire and missed!'

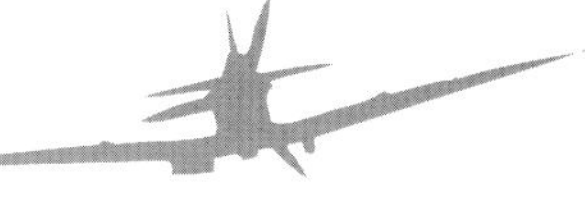

BELOW Mk VC AR501 has been a part of the Shuttleworth Collection since it was swapped by Loughborough Technical College for the Jet Provost prototype back in 1961! Built as one of a batch of 300 Mk Is and Vs by Westland, it was delivered to the RAF in June 1942. It served with four frontline units (and numerous OTUs) during its three years of service, with perhaps its first posting being its most memorable – flying with No 310 (Czech) Sqn, based at Exeter, in 1942/43 (*Denis Baldry*)

LEFT Whilst with the Czech squadron AR501 was assigned to the unit's OC, the legendary Frantisek 'Dolly' Dolezal – the aircraft has worn the latter's codes ever since its last major overhaul was completed in 1975. Soon after VE-Day the fighter was placed in storage at High Ercall with No 29 MU, before being bought by Loughborough Tech as an instructional airframe for its engineering students to repeatedly pull apart and rebuild. There its stayed until the aforementioned swap occurred in 1961

LEFT Like AR213, AR501 was chosen for restoration to airworthiness with the aid of money from United Artists following a survey on the fighter at Old Warden in 1967. Registered G-AWII, it logged over 50 hours of flying time during the filming of *The Battle of Britain*, after which it was stored again at RAE Thurleigh whilst money was raised to give it a more thorough overhaul. By 1973 sufficient funds had been collected, and AR501 was moved to Duxford, were a two-year rebuild was undertaken (*Denis Baldry*)

NN

LEFT Work was performed on a volunteer basis on AR501, and it wasn't until 27 June 1975 that it was finally flown again, with the late-lamented Neil Williams carrying out its test flights. One of the star attractions at Old Warden ever since, AR501 is maintained in 'working warbird' condition – lustreless paint scheme, original wartime reflector gunsight and accurate exhaust ejector stubs

RIGHT Flying AR501 throughout this chapter is Rolls-Royce Test Pilot, Andy Sephton. An ex-RAF Jaguar 'jock', and graduate of the EPTS School at Boscombe Down, Andy has been on the flying staff at Old Warden since 1992, and his mastery of the clipped-wing Spitfire is regularly displayed throughout the summer season at the 'cosy' Bedfordshire airfield. Indeed, the increased agility of the 'clipped, cropped and clapped' Mk VC make it ideally suited to the restricted airspace over the 'L-shaped' Old Warden site

INSET Elliptically-winged Mk VBs of No 91 'Nigeria' Sqn are fussed over at Hawkinge in May 1942. Known as the 'Jim Crow' specialists, the unit was tasked with intercepting low-level *Jagdwaffe* fighters indulging in 'tip and run' raids along the Channel coast. Strapped into the aircraft in the foreground ('DL-Z'/AB216) is squadron OC, 'Bobby' Oxspring, who finished the war with 13 kills

RIGHT The heavily-weathered wing leading edges and engine cowling fasteners often cause less than knowledgeable airshow attendees to complain that AR501 looks uncared for when compared with other UK-based Spitfires. Nothing could be further from the truth, however, as this machine is maintained in immaculate condition *internally*, where it matters most

RIGHT In keeping with AR501's 'frontline Fighter Command' feel, most of its pilots try and wear period headgear and overalls when flying the fighter. Andy Sephton is no exception, as he explains;

'I got in the habit of wearing a David Clark headset when flying David Pennell's LF IX MJ730. It didn't look very authentic, but the noise attenuation of that particular headset was excellent, and the noise in the Spitfire cockpit with the engine running has to be experienced to be believed. During World War 2, test pilots were issued with white leather helmets to the same pattern as fighter pilots of the era. I think that my David Clark offended Mr Pennell, as the rest of his aircraft is quite authentic and the modern form of head-dress did not match. So, with a smile, and characteristic generosity, he presented me with the white leather helmet you can see me wearing in these photographs, and handed it over with the following comment, "As you are a test pilot, you may as well look like one!" I've worn it ever since'

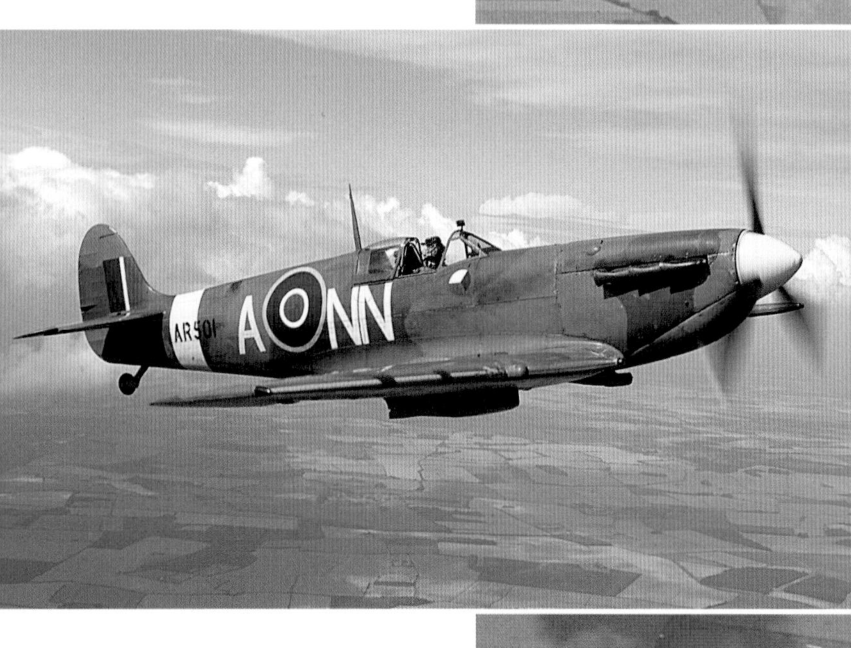

ABOVE *Cape Town II*, alias W3445, was just one a number of Mk Vs 'bought' by public subscription in 1941/42. Indeed, so popular was the 'buy a Spitfire' appeal that official instructions were issued by the RAF to groundcrews detailing just how big the inscription should be – no larger than four inches high – and that it should always be applied in yellow paint. Of course this order was often ignored, and flamboyant crests with flowing script appeared on presentation Spitfires. This particular machine had a chequered career in Fighter Command, entering service with No 611 Sqn in July 1941, and surviving a further four frontline tours – Nos 312 (twice), 91 and 317 Sqns – before seeing out its days with No 58 OTU. It was finally SoC on 17 July 1945 and unceremoniously scrapped

CHAPTER THREE

FAR EAST SPITFIRE

Spitfire LF Mk VIIIC MT719

Flight Lieutenant Don Healey
No 17 Sqn
1944 to 1946

'I arrived on No 17 Sqn in Burma having come from the Middle East, where I had flown Hurricane Mk IIs and Spitfire Mk Vs and VIIIs. By the time I turned up in-theatre the unit had been flying the Supermarine fighter for a few months. The old squadron pilots who had become attached to the venerable Hurricane since the early days of the Burma campaign were very impressed with the sleek Spitfire, one facet of the aircraft that they particularly appreciated being the LF Mk VIII's armament of two Hispano 20 mm cannon and two American 0.5 in Browning machine guns.

'The selection mechanism for choosing one or the other weapon in action could not have been easier, as on the spade grip in the cockpit, the fire selector button was vertically arranged on a rocker system. If you pressed the top part you got machine guns, if you pressed the bottom you got cannon, and if you pressed the middle you got the lot – this made the aircraft ideal for both ground-strafing and aerial combat.

'No 17 Sqn had spent until November 1944 working up on the Spitfire in Ceylon, and then was posted across to the Imphal Valley, in Burma, to help support the 14th Army's push into enemy territory. I flew with the unit from a variety of air strips down the length of Burma in the LF Mk VIII, ending up at Pegu (nicknamed "Pilsener"), just north of Rangoon, in late May 1945. Throughout this time our airfields in the main consisted of undrained and rolled out paddy fields – frequently flooded and muddy – which took a serious toll on our Spitfires.

'Fortunately, the Mk VIII was more robust than the earlier marks, and was better suited to "roughing it" on the jungle strips. However, like its more prolific stablemate, the Mk IX, it was powered by the

BELOW Flt Lt Don Healey strikes a pose alongside LF VIII 'YB-N', one of the many Spitfires he flew in combat over Burma in 1945. Although perhaps not the best quality photo in this volume, it nevertheless shows how basic the squadron dispersals were in-theatre – the runways were little better according to Don! (*Don Healey*)

ABOVE Although the carved out runways and dispersals were rough and ready when baked dry by the stifling heat, they were preferred to the quagmire caused when the rains came. These No 607 'County of Durham' Sqn pilots were photographed in the spring of 1945 struggling back to the debrief 'Basha' at Kalaywa following the completion of yet another army support sortie. No 17 Sqn Spitfire LF VIIIs were similarly adorned with white theatre bars by this late stage in the war

Merlin 66, with the supercharger unit at the rear of the engine block, which exuded vast amounts of heat when fired up and running. This wasn't a problem in the mild European climate at altitude, but in the stifling tropical heat over the Burmese jungle at medium- to low-level, the temperature in the cockpit was almost unbearable.

'Indeed, things were so bad that I had made a suggestion to "Doc" Watson, the unit's Rolls-Royce technical representative at the time, that his company should drill a hole in the wingtip of each new Spitfire, and channel a pipe down the length of the leading edge from the opening to the cockpit in order to blow cold air on the pilot's feet – needless to say "Doc's" bosses didn't adopt my suggestion! The only relief we got was by flying with the canopy slid back, which did marginally lower the cockpit temperature.

'Aside from the heat, the Mk VIII was a superb aeroplane to fly, possessing far greater horsepower with its two-speed/two-stage supercharger than the single-speed/single-stage Merlin 45 powered Mk V. However, the latter was a better "pilot's" aeroplane to fly, being more in balance than the Merlin 66 machines because of its better power-to-weight ratio. To do aerobatics in a Mk V was a pleasure, but to do them in a Mk VIII required more attention to what the aircraft was physically doing, as it could easily stall out in a slow speed roll due to its greater weight.

'However, if you got into a dogfight with Japanese Army Ki 43 "Oscar IIs", as we frequently did, the Mk VIII had two great plus points, should the enemy get astern of you: 1) you could out climb them if you could maintain a sustained ascent; and 2) if you had the height you could out dive them as well, as the Mk VIII weighed almost twice as much as any enemy fighter likely to be encountered. The manoeuvrability of the Nakajima fighter was well known by this stage in the war, and woe betide anyone who thought they could horizontally out-turn one in a Spitfire.

Dogfight

'On one memorable occasion a No 17 Sqn pilot had a Ki 43 lined up in his sights from dead astern, and as he went to press the fire button the "Oscar II" started to pull up sharply. He watched him continue to climb through the windscreen, over the top of the fuselage and out of sight to the Spitfire's rear. The next time he saw him was when he looked in his mirror and there he was sat right behind him! The pilot immediately adopted our favoured escape manoeuvre of pushing the stick forward and opening the throttle fully, followed by a boot-full of rudder so as to spiral the Spitfire vertically down in tights rolls, which we knew through past experience the Jap pilot couldn't hope to emulate.

'By this stage in the war an interception of a Japanese Army Air Force aircraft was a rare event, and during our lengthy tour of operations in Burma we only came across the enemy in the air on about half a dozen occasions. Our intelligence set up in Burma had become so advanced by 1945 that they could tell our Operations officer the night before if the enemy was expected to be encountered the following day. A typical scenario would see us tasked to patrol a bomb line over enemy territory at daybreak, with the rider from Ops that we were likely to meet Japanese aircraft at dawn. Sure enough, our section of Spitfires would duly intercept a number of bandits during the patrol.

'The intelligence network could predict Japanese fighter movements with almost 100 per cent accuracy by 1945 as Allied spotters in Burma would report sightings of aircraft being flown into Siam the preceding day, being fuelled up overnight, and then flown at low altitude over the hills that divided the two countries at dawn into our patrol area on fleeting anti-bomber sweeps. This routine was kept up by the Japanese until their final surrender. Such was the limited duration of their marauding patrols that you really had to be up in the air already to have any hope of intercepting them.

'Once combat had been joined, the best odds you could expect to see was a section of four Spitfires tackling a formation of 16 "Oscars" – they usually forayed over Burma in reasonable numbers. However, on 22 April 1945, Flg Off Ken Rutherford, DFC, RNZAF, ran into a formation of nine "Oscars" whilst returning from a patrol on his own – his wingman had earlier run low on fuel and been forced to return to base. With typical determination Ken tackled the enemy head on, and succeeded in downing the formation leader with an accurate burst of cannon fire. Having seen his demise, the remaining "Oscar" pilots quickly headed east for Siam – it was a good policy to let the enemy go once they had decided to form up and head home.

More kills

'Two days later Rutherford claimed one of a pair of Ki 43s shot down in the same area during a scrap with 10 Jap fighters. Two sections (four Spitfires in total) engaged the enemy over Toungoo at medium altitude, with Flt Lt B S "Tommy" Thompson bagging the second aircraft. However, Sgt D Crawford was shot down and killed in reply, having been bounced by a pair of "Oscars" at low altitude – he was the sole No 17 Sqn pilot killed in action during the Burma advance, and had only arrived on the squadron a few days before.

'Ironically, we had been stood down at Thedaw the day before this action took place in order to get the bulk of our weary Spitfires serviceable again, and being enterprising young fellows, us pilots had decided to take advantage of no flying for 72 hours by having a "pissy party". However, at 11 pm Ops rang up our OC, Sqn Ldr "Ginger" Lacey, and told him that a large formation of enemy aircraft was due over our sector at dawn. He explained that we had no aircraft fit to fly, but was curtly instructed that fellow Wing mates, No 152 Sqn, were also short of sufficient Spitfire VIIIs to engage the enemy.

BELOW Few pilots saw the remnants of the once invincible Japanese Army Air Force in the last year of the war in Burma, but one man who was involved in more than his fair share of aerial combat was Flt Lt Ken Rutherford, DFC, RNZAF. The victor over two 'Oscar IIs' in the space of ten days, Ken (seen here posing between his groundcrew), was No 17 Sqn's most successful pilot in terms of aerials kills with the LF VIII – the unit destroyed five aircraft (all Ki 43s) with the Spitfire (*Don Healey*)

ABOVE Pierced Steel Planking (PSP) solved many problems for the Allies in World War 2, and it is seen here providing a dispersal area for No 136 Sqn's LF VIIIs on Cocos Island in the summer of 1945. This veteran Burma unit was one of the first operators of the Mk VIII in-theatre, receiving new Spitfires in place of their war-weary Mk VBs in April 1944

'A frantic search was then made for four reasonably sober pilots, whilst the less than impressed groundcrews "burnt the midnight oil" in order to get sufficient aircraft ready for a pre-dawn launch. As it turned out, the resulting patrol saw some of the fiercest dogfighting experienced by the squadron during our second spell in Burma.

'Our last meeting with elements of the Japanese Army Air Force occurred on 29 April when a quartet of Spitfires returning from an uneventful patrol over Pegu encountered a sizeable formation of 16 "Oscar IIs" south of Toungoo. With barely 30 gallons of fuel each sloshing around in their tanks, the "lightweight" Mk VIIIs were led into the attack by A Flight boss, Flt Lt D C "Hawker" Hindley, who had also visually noted a pair of Nakajima fighters flying several hundred feet above the main formation in a top cover spread. As "Hawker" closed on the enemy, the two Ki 43s dived down on him from altitude, but these were quickly dealt with by Hindley's wingman, Plt Off R B Connell, who shot one down in short order.

'The dogfight that followed was in marked contrast to the engagement's fiery beginning. The remaining "Oscar IIs" milled around the constantly jinking and diving Spitfires, whose pilots were forced to fire short bursts at fleeting targets as they flashed across their bows during a rapid succession of high-g twists and turns. Eventually, the bulk of the enemy formation began to tire of this inconclusive dogfighting, and trailed off in ones and twos. However, the leader of the formation was obviously an "old head" for he remained in "hand-to-hand" combat with "Hawker" Hindley long after his subordinates had pushed off east for Siam. Indeed, Hindley had had the misfortune to latch onto this "Oscar II" right from the initial interception, and could barely do enough to stay with his opponent as he proceeded to perform a series of stunning aerobatic manoeuvres in his nimble Nakajima.

'Finally, after carrying out six consecutive gunnery attacks without managing to fire a conclusive burst due to the Jap pilot continually out-turning him, Hindley gave up and headed for home, with barely 15 gallons of fuel showing on his gauges. The "Oscar" pilot followed suit.

'Taking on fighters was the exception to the daily task of ground-controlled target strafing in support of the army. This usually took the form of a man in a jeep up at the frontline guiding us in by radio to hit all manner of targets. On one particularly memorable sortie, I was in a two-aircraft section with Flt Lt Ted Marshal, DFC – an Australian who commanded B Flight – and he spotted a recently re-roofed "basha" (hut) on the edge of the jungle whilst on patrol. Marshal was a very experienced tactical recon pilot and could see things moving under the jungle canopy better than anyone on No 17 Sqn – he even adapted his flying "outlook" to facilitate target spotting. This meant he kept his eyes on the ground at all times, leaving me to handle the sky above the horizon.

'On the mission in question, we each took it in turns to strafe the hut, trying to set it on fire, and on my second pass the grass roof slid back and I came face to face with a multi-barrelled pom-pom anti-aircraft gun! Just as they took aim to fire, my starboard cannon seized and the recoil from the still-firing port 20 mm threw the Spitfire into a side-slip to the right and I skidded sideways barely 10 ft over the top of the hut. This involuntary manoeuvre obviously put the Jap gunners off their aim as they missed me by some margin – I could see their astonished faces as I sped over the top of the "basha", and no doubt they could see my equalling wide-eyed gaze through the canopy!

'I climbed back up to 2000 ft and reported my sighting to Ted, who suggested returning to Meiktila to inform our dive-bombing friends in No 28 Sqn of our discovery. They duly scrambled a dozen Hurricane IICs and we guided them back to the target, which they destroyed.

'With our mix of cannon and heavy calibre machine guns, we were always in demand to help clear stubborn ground forces from the path of the 14th Army. The Spitfire carried enough ammunition for a minute-and-a-half length burst, which may not seem like a lot. However, it is amazing the effect a well-aimed short squirt had on the Japanese. We would always fit a few tracer rounds in the magazines about 50 shells from the end of ammunition supply in order to tell us how much we had left in each gun. Japanese fighter pilots soon cottoned on to this during aerial duels, and due to their invariably superior numbers, would jump on the first man to fire tracer. Our response was to get the squadron armourers to feed tracer into our ammo belts several rounds into our supply, which certainly caught a number of "Oscar" pilots out!

Meiktila

'As the front moved further south towards Mandalay during April 1945, we started flying down from our base at Ywadon to operate during the day from a forward strip 100 miles away at Meiktila, which was the scene of some very fierce battles – over 5000 Japanese troops were killed during the struggle for control of this strategic area. Two sections of two aircraft would head for Meiktila before dawn, and whilst a pair would journey out on patrol over the bomb-line once over the battle zone, the remaining Spitfires would be employed strafing Japanese positions immediately around the strip in order to help the RAF Regiment on the ground secure the airfield. Every night for about three weeks, Japanese commandos would take control of Meiktila's dirt runway until beaten back into the jungle at dawn by Allied troops breaking out of their "defensive box".

'Once the strip had been recaptured, the dead Japanese that lay strewn across the site were cleared off, and the pilots quickly given the signal to land. Once on the ground the aircraft would re-arm and refuel, and then wait for the section on patrol to return. After two hours the Spitfires would duly appear overhead, and the pair on the ground would take-off and head out on patrol, leaving the recently arrived fighters to take their place at Meiktila to refuel and re-arm. This routine continued throughout the day until dusk began to draw in, and we would then head back north to Ywadon, whilst the troops on the ground would return to the security of their defensive box, leaving the Japanese to swarm over the airstrip once again.

'During the Battle of Meiktila, the Japanese troops collected scalps from dead Gurkhas as trophies, so the Gurkhas retaliated by lopping off the heads of the Japanese dead and mixing them in a pile. This demoralised the enemy, who believed that without their heads their ancestors would not recognise them in heaven. The Gurkhas shaved their heads in response to the outbreak of scalping, leaving just a tuft of hair on the crown so that Allah could lift them up to heaven after they were killed! "Ginger" Lacey, and the remainder of No 17 Sqn, did the same as a tribute to the Ghurkhas, who guarded us at Meiktila.

'As we moved further south into Burma, our sup-

BELOW No 17 Sqn suffered a terrible attrition rate whilst fighting its way back down into Burma in 1945, although by this stage in the war replacement aircraft were always available back in India. Poor runways were often a pilot's undoing, the Spitfire's notoriously delicate undercarriage failing to endure the rigours of operating from jungle strips. This LF VIII ground-looped soon after landing at Ywadon in the spring of 1945, and was quickly stripped of its usable parts and then dumped (*Don Healey*)

ABOVE LV648 is carefully marshalled out from its dispersal at a maintenance unit in Calcutta prior to performing a post-reassembly check flight in January 1944. Like all other Spitfires in-theatre, this machine had been test flown in Britain soon after its construction, then crated up and shipped out to India. Service records for many SEAC Spitfires are sketchy, to say the least, and the history of this F VIII remains a mystery, other than it was initially issued to No 67 Sqn at Chittagong in February 1944, and was eventually SoC on 27 March 1947

ply line got severely stretched, and we began to suffer serious unserviceability due to the lack of small, but crucial, parts. One particular problem centred around the rubber pressure seals in the undercarriage actuators perishing in the heat, and thus stopping the gear from retracting. We ended up with eight Spitfires grounded because of a lack of seals, but the solution to this problem came from an unlikely source.

'As our forces continued advancing they would regularly overrun Japanese Army hospitals, and our Medical Officer, Dr Fred Jackson (known to all and sundry as "Mad Jack the Jungle Quack" due to his extended stay in the Far East), would regularly seek out these sites in search of medical supplies.

'On one occasion he brought back with him some cartons full of Jap condoms without teats, and upon opening the contents up, we found that they were made of rubber that was the consistency of a bicycle tube – very insensitive these Japs! When rolled up they formed a solid disc which one of our flight sergeants ("Digger" Lee) thought would fit in the troublesome oleo legs, and act as the perfect substitute seal.

'I happened to be squadron test pilot that week, and he asked me to fly each of these "repaired" Spitfires in turn, claiming that he had received the appropriate parts from India. Each machine checked out, and I said to him afterwards that I couldn't remember any spares being flown in. It was only then that the flight sergeant came clean about the condoms, and from that moment on we would say that every time our wheels went up and down it was by courtesy of the Japanese Medical Services!

'Because of the rough nature of our airstrips, and constant flying at full throttle, a Spitfire rarely lasted more than six weeks in the frontline, with undercarriage failure, and the resulting ground loop, being one of the major wreckers of aircraft. If a machine saw more than two months' service with us, it was doing well – we also got through engines at an alarming rate.

'I only began to realise how many aircraft we went through many years after the war when I was trying to tie up serials in logbooks with squadron maintenance records – we had five "YB-Ts" in as many months! At the time one didn't really think too much about how hard Burma was on Spitfires.

'I flew a total of about 600 hours on Spitfires, and quite a bit on Hurricanes too. Much of this was on operations – indeed on one single day I completed nine hours and ten minutes at the controls, divided between five patrols. This figure does not include 30 minutes either way from the airstrip at Ywadon to the Japanese frontline at Meiktila and back – we didn't log this as operational flying. The average endurance in a Mk VIII was about two-and-a-half hours, without overload tanks.

'At war's end the surviving RAF Mk VIIIs were sold off to the Indian Air Force, and it was only because of this sale that we have some of this mark still with us today.'

YB J
MT719

ABOVE AND LEFT Outside the RAF, the greatest employer of the Mk VIII was the RAAF, which received no less than 410 aircraft as replacements for the earlier Mk VCs supplied from the UK in 1942. Delivered between November 1943 and June 1945, the Spitfires saw much service both defending Australia and as part of No 80 Wing, chasing the Japanese back across the Pacific from island to island. The top photo shows a five-ship formation of LF VIIIs on a training flight over New South Wales in mid-1945, their lack of squadron code letters indicating their employment by a second-line OTU. The shot on the left shows an anonymous pilot climbing out of a well-used LF VIII (A58-518 in RAAF service, MT618 when built) following the completion of a routine patrol from Livingstone, south of Darwin, in mid-1944. This machine was eventually lost without a trace during a fighter sweep over the jungle of north-east Borneo in July 1945

PAGES 70 AND 71, ABOVE AND LEFT The LF VIII is considered to be one of the best looking of all the various marks of Spitfire, as these shots clearly show. MT719 was a one squadron machine when it served with the RAF, flying solely with No 17 Sqn in Burma in 1944/45. It had been shipped out to India in July 1944, and following its reconstruction, was allocated to the unit late in the year, as Don Healey explains;

'MT719 had arrived on the squadron from Bombay in late 1944, being flown over to Burma by Flt Sgt Rex de Silva, the unit's sole Ceylonese pilot – it made such an impression on him that he noted in his logbook, "I picked up the new 'J' today, coded MT719, and what a red hot machine it is!" He proceeded to fly it with A Flight for a number of weeks. By May, it was fairly knackered, as Rex noted in his log – "Poor old 'J' is coming to the end of its life, having refused to start this morning"'

RIGHT Don Healey continues;

'At about this time the fighter went to No 3 Repair and Salvage Unit and had its old Merlin swapped for a new one. It was still sitting here when I arrived back from Rangoon, having represented No 17 Sqn in the victory march through the Burmese capital whilst the unit was at Pegu. Upon my return to the latter I discovered that the squadron had flown to Madura, in India, to convert to Mk XIVs. No 909 Wing boss, Grp Capt Donald Finlay, had also taken part in the march, and he told all 13 of us pilots from various squadrons who had been left behind to represent the RAF in the procession, to grab an aircraft each from the Repair and Salvage Unit – they had Spitfires, Hurricanes, Beaufighters, Hurricanes, Mosquitos and Thunderbolts – and fly back to India – I chose MT719. Our "rag tag" air force duly left Burma, and at each refuelling stop someone got left behind due to a technical snag – a fate which eventually struck me down at Vishahkhaptnam when I suffered carburettor problems. I was accommodated in the Sultan's palace for several days while we found someone to adjust the engine, and then I pressed on to Madura.'

Following its discarding by the RAF, MT719 passed into the hands of the Indian Air Force. It remained in their possession until bought at auction (along with seven other Spitfires) in 1977 by the late Ormond Hayden-Baillie and his brother Wensley. Despite Ormond's death later that same year in a P-51 crash, MT719 was still brought back to the UK, although it was soon sold in an unrestored state to Franco Actis, and shipped to Turin. Restored by a team led by Paul Mercer, MT719's previous identity was discovered during its stripping to bare metal – it was covered by six coats of paint! Test flown by Sqn Ldr Paul Day in October 1982, MT719 was displayed in Italy until Aircraft Investments brought it back to the UK in 1988. The Spitfire was bought in 1993 by Jim Cavanaugh, and is maintained in airworthy condition at his Flight Museum at Addison Airport in Dallas, Texas.

Wg Cdr Al Sheppard is the pilot of MT719 throughout this chapter

MT719

CHAPTER FOUR

THE MERCURIAL MK IX

Spitfire LF Mk IXCs MH434 and MK732, LF Mk IXEs ML417 and TE566, and T.9s ML407 and PV202

Squadron Leader Pete Brothers
Hornchurch Wing
June-July 1942

'The first Mk IX I flew was when I served briefly with the Hornchurch Wing as acting wing leader in late June 1942, prior to going to No 602 Sqn. I was all set to begrudgingly head "downunder" with my Australian squadron when I was taken off the boat and sent to Essex instead! The Hornchurch Wing leader, Wg Cdr Peter Powell (a 1940 Hurricane ace with No 111 Sqn, Ed.), had been wounded in combat and was off ops, so I was drafted in as temporary replacement due to my recent Circus experience with the Kenley Wing.

'One of the trio of units then at Hornchurch was No 64 Sqn, commanded by seasoned Spitfire ace Sqn Ldr Wilfred Duncan-Smith. His unit was the first at Hornchurch to replace its Mk VBs with the urgently needed Mk IX, and I was fortunate enough to fly several sorties in one of these factory-fresh machines.

'The two-stage, two-speed, supercharger of the Mk 61 Merlin was a revelation, with the former coming in with a bang at an altitude of about 16,000 ft. One drawback of the new machine, however, was that it could be tipped on its nose more easily, due to the centre of gravity having shifted forward because of the elongated engine nacelle required to house the "blown" Merlin.

'Indeed, a lot of pilots claimed that the Mk IX was the best Spitfire of the war, but I'm afraid I have to disagree on that point. For me the Griffon-engined Mk XIV was clearly superior to all other wartime variants, and fortunately Spitfire test pilot Jeffrey Quill agrees with me!'

BELOW An impressive nine-ship flyby of factory-fresh Mk IXs heralds the arrival of a recently re-equipped squadron at an anonymous fighter station in No 11 Group in 1943

Wing Commander Alan Deere
supernumerary with No 611 Sqn,
then Biggin Hill Wing Leader
February 1943 to September 1943

'In February 1943 I saw my chance to take a step forward. "Daddy" Bouchier, now an Air Commodore, arrived at No 13 Group headquarters as SASO (Senior Air Staff Officer), and I appealed to him to allow me a two weeks' attachment at Biggin Hill, where "Sailor" Malan (ex-No 74 Sqn ace, Ed.) was now installed as Station Commander. "After all", I pleaded, "an air staff officer must keep up to date with current operations". I knew I could fix it with "Sailor" – in fact, I had already got his verbal agreement – and it was merely a question of being allowed away from the Group for two weeks. I think memories of No 54 Sqn and Hornchurch in 1940 won the day, for "Daddy" gave his consent.

'At Biggin Hill, Dicky Milne (an ace on both Hurricanes and Spitfires, Ed.), who was the Wing Leader, arranged for me to fly as a member of No 611 Sqn (which had just lost its popular Australian CO, Sqn Ldr Hugo 'Sinker' Armstrong, shot down and killed by Fw 190 *'Experten'* Ofz Heinz Gomann of II./JG 26 on a sweep over the Channel on 5 February – one of three No 611 Sqn pilots lost on this sortie, 'Sinker' had claimed 10.5 kills up to his death. He was replaced by Sqn Ldr Charlton 'Wag' Haw – 4.5 kills – who had been serving as a flight commander with No 122 Sqn at Hornchurch since May 1942. His Mk IX experience was to prove invaluable at No 611 Sqn, Ed.). I knew how squadron commanders hated supernumeraries in their unit, and I was careful therefore not to stake my claims to leadership, but to fly when, and in whatever position in the formation the squadron commander, or his flight commanders, wished. As a result, I found myself flying as a number two, as a number three and in any stooge position in the squadron where there was a gap to be filled. To be frank, I can't say I was happy going through the mill again, as it were, especially having been a leader since the early days of the war. Nevertheless, I was exhilarated, in a curious sort of way, for the first time since the fateful day over Le Touquet with No 403 Sqn (Deere's Canadian outfit had been bounced on a sweep over France on 2 June 1942 by a particularly aggressive formation of 30+ Fw 190s, and eight Spitfire Mk VBs and six pilots had been lost, Ed.).

'At all costs I had to bag myself a Hun; somehow I felt that a flying appointment depended on it. When my 14 days were up I hadn't fired a shot in anger. The weather had been bad throughout the period, and the wing had been on only a few abortive shows. On two occasions I managed to get myself on a Rhubarb (that useless and hated operation) but even then without success; although on one occasion, when flying as a number three in a section of four, we did manage to surprise some Fw 190s but we were not quick enough to catch them and, using their superior speed at low-level, they avoided combat.

'With "Sailor's" connivance I decided to stay on for a few more days and risk the wrath of "Daddy" on my return to No 13 Group. Two days later (on 16 February 1943, Ed.) I was in combat. I was leading a section in the wing when at 37,000 ft over St Omer I sighted a dozen Fw 190s some 10,000 ft below. I called Dicky Milne and told him I was taking my section down to attack. As we neared the enemy fighters they saw us and split. I singled out one, determined at all costs to get him. I had speed and height in my favour and, in contrast to the ill-fated battle with No 403 Sqn, I was behind the controls of a Spitfire IX (F Mk IXC BS556 to be exact, a Merlin 61-engined Mk V airframe that was amongst the first 'Mk IXs' so designated – amazingly, this machine survived four frontline tours, a spell in Training Command and two Cat C accidents, before being struck off charge and sold for scrap in 1949, Ed.), which was superior to the Fw 190 above 25,000 ft.

'To me, the fight that ensued was more important than any that had gone before – my future was at stake. I felt like a boxer entering the ring before a big fight, tense and breathless, and curiously excited. As my cannons found their mark, and bits from the disintegrating Focke-Wulf hurtled past my aircraft, there was no exhilaration at victory, no sorrow at killing, no revenge for past hurts, but merely a sense of achievement – this is what I had set out to do, and I had done it. "Sailor" was delighted at my success. After two more uneventful days at Biggin, I was ordered to return north to No 13 Group.'

Wing Leader

This one-off success had the desired affect on the senior officers in Fighter Command, as just when Alan Deere had thought his chance of commanding a wing had passed, he was told by 'Daddy' Bouchier that he was to take on the Kenley Wing in the frontline No 11 Group sector. However, prior to him taking up his new post with the all-Canadian wing in

Surrey, Biggin Wing Leader Dickie Milne was shot down into the Channel by a Fw 190A-4 of II./JG 26 and captured on 14 March 1943, following a bitter dogfight over Berck-sur-Mer.

Elements of this crack *Gruppe*, commanded by Adolf Galland's brother, Hptm Wilhelm-Ferdinand 'Wutz' Galland, also bagged two other Spitfires during this one-sided skirmish without suffering any losses – one flown by a supernumerary Wing Commander by the name of Slater and the other by newly-appointed No 340 Sqn CO, Comdt Reilhac, who had only just filled the position left vacant by Capt Schloesing, lost again to II./JG 26 four weeks before. It was very much a demoralised Biggin Hill Wing that welcomed the veteran Kiwi ace in late March – the Kenley position, meanwhile, had been filled by newly-promoted Wg Cdr J E 'Johnnie' Johnson. Alan Deere continues;

'I was now all set to renew acquaintances with the formidable Focke-Wulfs, but this time I was better equipped. The Biggin Hill squadrons (Nos 611 and 341 Sqns) were using the Spitfire IXBs (actually officially known as LF IXCs, and fitted with the Merlin 66 engine – squadron pilots referred to this mark as the 'Mk IXB', and christened the F IXC the 'Mk IXA', the latter being powered by a Merlin 61, 63 or 63A engine, Ed.), a mark of Spitfire markedly superior in performance to the Fw 190A below 27,000 ft. Unlike the Spitfire IXA, with which all other Spitfire IX wings in the Group were equipped, the IXB's supercharger came in at a lower altitude and the aircraft attained its best performance at 21,000 ft, or at roughly the same altitude as the Fw 190. At this height it was approximately 30 mph faster, was better in the climb and vastly more manoeuvrable. As an all-round fighter the Spitfire IXB was supreme, and undoubtedly the best mark of Spitfire produced, despite later and more powerful versions. The call-sign allocated to me as wing leader was "Brutus".

'In the spring the first *Gruppe* of the *Richtofen Geschwader* (I./JG 2) had moved into Trocqueville airfield, just south of the Seine Estuary, under the command of well-known fighter ace, Maj Walter Oesau. As soon as I learned of this I telephoned Johnny Walker, who was responsible for planning operations at No 11 Group, to ask if we could plan a wing show to Trocqueville airfield with the object of enticing this *Gruppe* into the air. He readily agreed.'

Deere's plan called for a surprise attack on the airfield from a low-level approach, in the hope that the Fw 190 pilots would be caught taxying their aircraft into position for take-off. No 611 Sqn was tasked with attacking the site, whilst the Free-French-manned No 341 Sqn would patrol to the south of the airfield at 3000 ft, guarding against a surprise bounce by other elements of I./JG 2 based at Evereux.

ABOVE Despite bearing the inscription *HEH NIZAM'S STATE RAILWAY No 2*, the identity of this Mk IX, and its young Polish pilot, remain a mystery. The latter's attire is typical of that worn by Fighter Command pilots during the late war years in the west

'I first sighted the airfield when we were about five miles from it. At the same moment René Mouchotte's voice, unruffled as always, came over the R/T:

'"Brutus, there are aircraft taxying on the airfield."

'From a higher vantage point René had a better view than I, but a few seconds later I saw them, visible mainly because of the sun glinting on perspex hoods as they taxied into position for take-off. But we too had been spotted – bursting red flares appeared over the airfield as a warning to the Hun pilots of danger, and they reacted instantly. Before we could get in range the aircraft were airborne and had disappeared in several directions at low-level, lost to sight against the wooded background of the surrounding countryside. We were still about a mile away, and there was no point in opening fire. I cursed our bad luck – ten seconds sooner and we would have caught them with their pants down. As it was there was only the empty airfield and a miserable-looking hangar to fire at, the latter receiving a burst from me as I hurtled across in pursuit.

'"Brutus from Grass-seed. Enemy aircraft coming

up fast from the south, about 5000 ft." René's voice broke through on the R/T.

'Veering right and climbing, I answered. "Ok, Grass-seed, coming up to assist."

'We met them head on in the climb, and a glorious dogfight developed, reminiscent of my first encounter with the Hun over Calais/Marck. This time, however, we were evenly matched in numbers. The danger from collision was greater than from Hun bullets as Spitfires and Focke-Wulfs wove a chaotic pattern in the congested air space over the airfield. It was impossible to hold one's fire for more than a fleeting second without being attacked – one moment I found myself diving vertically at the ground after a retreating Hun, and the next my over-revving airscrew was clawing at the air in response to my full throttle demand as I endeavoured to spiral upwards out of range of an attacker. This time there was to be no sudden clearance of the sky, for the Huns were obviously determined to fight it out. But our petrol was running low and we had a long way to go before clearing enemy territory. I therefore gave the order to withdraw.

'"Brutus calling all Turban and Grass-seed aircraft. Withdraw to R/V point immediately."

'We had planned a rendezvous point just off Fecamp on the coast and I now set course for there with Flg Off Paddy Neal, my number two, in attendance. At Fecamp, I was eventually joined by the majority of No 611 Sqn, but No 341 Sqn made their way home independently.'

Honours even

Once back in Kent it was discovered that I./JG 2 and the Biggin Hill Wing had both scored two kills apiece, No 611 Sqn claiming both victories, whilst No 341 Sqn lost a pair of Spitfires – the latter had been downed during the initial bounce by the Evereux Fw 190s, which had dived headlong through the Free French squadron into Johnny Checketts' unit.

On 4 May Alan Deere led both his squadrons on a bomber escort mission for a formation of 79 B-17Fs attacking the Ford and General motor works at Antwerp. This raid was a precursor to the much larger strikes flown by the Eighth Air Force deep into Germany in 1944/45, and due to its relatively short radius of action, two Fighter Command wings ('Johnnie' Johnson's Kenley Wing was the second RAF outfit involved) were draughted in to help the USAAF's six newly-transitioned P-47 squadrons provide bomber escort.

Up to this point Flying Fortress missions had been flown into Europe with just short range support seeing the bombers escorted barely into France. For the bulk of the mission they were on their own, and losses had been horrendous. However, on this occasion, the protection of a dozen fighter squadrons ensured no losses were inflicted on the B-17Fs of the 91st, 303rd, 305th and 306th Bomb Groups – the *Jagdflieger*, however, were not so fortunate, as Alan Deere recounts in the following passage;

'Groping flak followed us to the target, largely ineffective at 25,000 ft, but there were no enemy fighters in the area – a diversionary Fortress "spoof" had been laid on to the south and this no doubt accounted for their absence. Over the islands of Walcheren on the return journey a formation of Focke-Wulfs appeared to the north and begun a desultory series of attacks, only to be met by the eager freelancing Spitfires forming the close escort. Two dived across my line of fire and I whipped into the attack, only to find myself frighteningly and unexpectedly immersed in a deluge of tracer from the starboard box of Fortresses. The angle was such that they had little chance of hitting me, or the Hun, and I continued my chase. Here was my chance of a first kill as wing leader. Closing rapidly from dead astern and slightly below, I steadied my aim and pressed the firing button, continuing firing as the range shortened to within 150 yards. Dancing splodges of yellow along the enemy's fuselage signified success. The Fw 190 wobbled under the impact, comically it seemed, burst into flames and dived away to destruction.'

Wing Commander 'Sammy' Sampson
Wing Leader No 145 'Free French' Wing
January to August 1945

'On the morning of 13 March 1945 we were scheduled to escort 54 Mitchell bombers who were to attack the Lengerich marshalling yards. The bombers were in three boxes of 18, and No 340 Sqn with me leading, was the only escort of the last group, themselves flying in three boxes of six.

'After the Mitchells had dropped their bombs the first boxes opened their throttles and there was soon a gap of some three miles between the first two and the last box. I instructed Commandant Massart and his Yellow Section to stay behind and guard the bombers, whilst the other two sections and I stayed between the first and second box.

'Massart then called up to say they were under attack by a dozen Bf 109Gs, so I told him I would turn to help them, leaving one section with the leading 12 bombers. I could see a general meleé in progress as I approached and, horror of horrors, I heard Massart say that he had been badly hit and was going to have to bale out. As I closed in I was able to see the 109 still firing at Massart and began to line up the Messerschmitt in my gyro gunsight at 800 yards.

'When I was at 600 yards, the German pilot saw me, and turned in my direction. I gave him a short burst of all my armament, having got him in my gunsight with both the "+" and the movable "dot" together. To my surprise I saw a strike on the front of his fighter which seemed to knock him off balance because he then turned hard towards me and my immediate reaction was, "You've had it, boy".

'I easily out-turned him and got on his tail. I was still firing when the pilot baled out, but I had the feeling he was hit, then the 109 disintegrated. By this time I was so close that my Spitfire was hit and slightly damaged by Hun debris, but it caused no serious problems. Needless to say I was very impressed with the gyroscopic gunsight and I wished I could have had it at the time of the Dieppe Raid.'

Gyro Gunsight

In his volume *Late Marque Spitfire Aces 1942-45* (published by Osprey in 1995), Dr Alfred Price detailed just how the Mk II Gyro Gunsight, developed by the Royal Aircraft Establishment at Farnborough, and put to good effect by 'Sammy' Sampson to achieve his fourth (and last) kill of the war, worked in combat;

'This device was a great improvement over the GM 2 reflector sight, and operated on the principal that if a fighter pilot followed an enemy aircraft in the turn and held his gunsight on the latter, his rate of turn was proportional to the deflection angle required to hit the target. A gyroscope measured his rate of turn, and tilted a mirror which moved the position of the sighting graticule to show the required deflection angle. The required deflection varied with range, however, so the gunsight incorporated a simple system of optical rangefinding. Before the engagement the pilot set on the sight the approximate wingspan of the enemy aircraft. As he closed on his foe, the pilot operated a control mounted on the throttle arm which altered the diameter of the sighting graticule so that its size matched the wingspan of the enemy aircraft. Since the wingspan of the target aircraft had been set on the sight, the adjustment of the graticule "told" the gunsight the range of the target. An analogue computer in the gunsight worked out the correct point ahead of the target at which the pilot should aim in order to score hits.

'Once fighter pilots got used to the new sight, and learned its foibles, the general accuracy of deflection shooting improved dramatically. During 1944 an analysis of 130 combats by Spitfire Mk IXs fitted with fixed-graticule sights revealed that there had been 34 kills – 26 per cent of the total. During the same period, one squadron operating the same Spitfire variant fitted with the new gunsight took part in 38 combats, scoring 19 kills – 50 per cent of the total. The new gunsight virtually doubled the effectiveness of air-to-air gunnery. With the new sight, pilots reported scoring hits on evading targets at ranges as great as 600 yards, and at deflection angles of up to 50°.'

'Sammy' scored his final kill in his much-cherished 'SS'-coded LF Mk IXC (like other pilots of the period, he refers to this fighter as a 'Mk IXB' in his

LEFT Unlike the anonymous Pole on the previous spread, there is no doubting the identity of this Fighter Command veteran – Wg Cdr R W F 'Sammy' Sampson. He is seen here in 1943 sat astride his Mk VB whilst serving as a flight commander with No 131 Sqn in 1943 (*'Sammy' Sampson*)

ABOVE Two classic fighters, same engine! No 43 Sqn LF IX MK118 is refuelled at the Anzio beach-head in mid-1944 whilst a Twelfth AF P-51C Mustang awaits the return of its pilot

excellent autobiography *Spitfire Offensive*, written in conjunction with Norman Franks in 1994), although the rest of his four-squadron strong wing were by this time flying LF Mk XVIs. He continues;

'Although the Wing was mainly equipped with Spitfire XVIs, I liked to fly the Spitfire IXB. Unfortunately the airfield commander had overhead some of my French pilots saying that they found it difficult to keep up with me sometimes in their Mk XVIs, so I was quietly asked to change my IXB for a XVI.

'With the Mk IXA (a F Mk IXC, Ed.) and IXB, we had an aircraft designed to operate in excess of 30,000 ft where it had the edge on both the Messerschmitts and Focke-Wulfs. Unfortunately, when it came into full use in 1943, operational heights seldom reached beyond 25,000 ft. The IXB was in full use by 1944, it had all the answers and was superior in all conditions to the German day fighters.

'The Mk XVI, which equipped the Wing in February 1945, was said to be the same as the IXB with the exception that the Merlin 66 engine was produced in the USA by Packard. The AFDU (Air Fighting Development Unit), now under Air Commodore Dick Atcherley (who had scored three kills in North Africa flying Beaufighters with No 25 Sqn, Ed.), with Wg Cdr Francis Blackadder, DSO (a Battle of Britain Hurricane ace, Ed.), as I/C Flying, received a report from me disagreeing with their findings that there was no no difference between the Merlin 66 produced in the UK and that produced by Packard. As I was so adamant, Drope Station Commander, Grp Capt Loel Guiness, arranged for one of the engineers from Rolls-Royce, Derby, to visit us and I expressed my opinion forcibly. The engineer told us that over the period there had been very many minor alterations to the original Blue Print, which all the production team understood. The fact that the Blue Print had been sent to the US, showing none of these minor adjustments, might possibly make a slight difference. He also, rather with his tongue in cheek, suggested that as a Wing Leader, my IXB probably received much more polish which would make a difference. I made a somewhat rude response.'

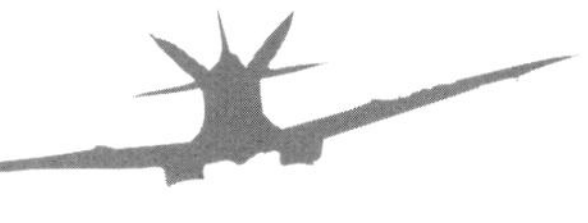

ABOVE Arguably one of the more famous Spitfire in the world is LF IXC MH434, which has been maintained in airworthy condition ever since it came off the line at Castle Bromwich in August 1943. It has worn many schemes over the decades, and seen combat with both the RAF and Dutch Air Force. Since 1983 it has resided at Duxford with The Old Flying Machine Company (OFMC), where it is rightly regarded by father and son Ray and Mark Hanna as 'the jewel in their crown'

LEFT Temporarily back in Kent after an endless succession of combat sweeps over Normandy, a Norwegian pilot keeps an eye on proceedings as his urgent 'cargo' is readied for the short 'Channel hop' back to France in July 1944. When filled with fuel, the centreline external tank greatly increased the Spitfire IX's loiter time over the frontline

LEFT Wearing spurious squadron codes (the letters 'WO' were actually worn by No 90 Sqn Fortress Is in 1941!) applied for the filming of a BBC television series at Duxford in the summer of 1995, MH434 formates with the similarly-marked Spitfire PR XI PL965 high over Cambridgeshire in October of the same year

ABOVE In 1988 MH434 was one of six Spitfires used in the making of the controversial London Weekend Television (LWT) series *Piece of Cake* – indeed the OFMC acted as both aerial directors and technical consultants to LWT during the filming of the drama. In order to make the late-war Spitfires appear more like the Mk Is of 1940 that they were supposed to be representing, all six machines donned the appropriate day fighter scheme of the period. Although the remaining Spitfires soon returned to more authentic grey/green shades after the shooting was completed, MH434 retained its brown and green scheme for a number of years, making it particularly appealing to airshow organisers celebrating the 50th anniversary year of the Battle of Britain in 1990. Seen here departing Duxford with Alan Walker at the controls, MH434 has had the 'AV' codes of No 121 'Eagle' Sqn added, as well as a Fighter Command fuselage band

LEFT A clipped-wing Spitfire LF IXE of No 132 Sqn awaits its load of two 250-lb bombs and a single 500-lb weapon in this staged photo taken at the imaginatively named B11 airfield in Normandy in August 1944. One of the first units to land in France, No 132 Sqn was tasked with close-support work over the frontline until its posting back to England in September

LEFT This photograph was taken in the same month as the previous image, and shows elliptically-winged 'LE-Q'/EN974 of No 242 Sqn taxying to a refuelling point at Calenzana, on Corsica, prior to performing a sweep over the *Anvil-Dragoon* invasion beaches in southern France

ABOVE The 20 mm cannon barrels (and associated wing blisters) and the rounded fin tip help distinguish MH434 from PR XI PL965 in this atmospheric twilight shot taken in October 1995. Note also that the former has a fixed tailwheel identical to its close-cousin, the Mk V. Brian Smith is flying the Mk IX and Rod Dean the Mk XI on this occasion

RIGHT An informal group shot of No 349 'Belgian' Sqn's entire pilot strength, taken during a rare stand down between close-support missions in France in the early autumn of 1944. The squadron 'prop' is Spitfire Mk IX MJ360

B

LEFT Mark Hanna makes a 'gunnery' pass at the hapless photo-ship over Cambridgeshire. Having spent a number of years masquerading as an early-mark Spitfire, MH434 was resprayed in its correct August 1943 No 222 'Natal' Sqn scheme in time for the aircraft's 50 birthday celebrations, held at Duxford on 25 July 1993

LEFT AND RIGHT Whilst in service with No 222 Sqn at Hornchurch, MH434 was flown mainly by ex-Malta Hurricane ace, Flt Lt Henry 'Pat' Lardner-Burke, DFC. A South African who had joined the RAF in 1940, he was initially posted to No 19 Sqn at Duxford upon completing his conversion onto Spitfires at No 57 OTU in early 1941. However, before he could see action with the unit, he was posted to Hurricane-equipped No 46 Sqn, and sent off to Malta.

During the summer of that year, Lardner-Burke's squadron was heavily involved in repelling repeated attacks by the Italian *Regia Aeronautica* as they attempted to bomb the island into submission. By November he had claimed five kills (four C.200s and a solitary C.202), but moments after making 'ace' he was badly wounded when a 12.7 mm bullet from an Italian fighter penetrated his seat armour and passed clean through his chest, puncturing a lung in the process. Somehow he managed to land on Malta, and was sent back to England.

Following a spell as a gunnery instructor at Sutton Bridge, he returned to the frontline with a posting to No 222 Sqn as a flight commander, then based at Rochford, in March 1943. Within two months of his arrival the unit had replaced its Mk VBs with Mk IXs, and were performing sweeps over France with the Hornchurch Wing. MH434 turned up at the Essex fighter station on 19 August 1943, and was immediately 'acquired' by Lardner-Burke, who christened it *Mylcraine*, and had his groundcrew apply his 'scoreboard' beneath the cockpit on the port side. The South African soon added to his score, downing one Fw 190 and damaging a second whilst part of a Ramrod escort for Eighth AF B-17s over St Omer on 27 August. A second Fw 190 kill was achieved over Nieuport nine days later, and his (and MH434's) final claim was logged on 8 September when he shared in the destruction of a Bf 109G over northern France.

'Pat' Lardner-Burke left MH434, and No 222 Sqn, following a posting to HQ Fighter Command in October 1943. He survived the war, and eventually retired from the RAF with the rank of Wing Commander. Sadly, he died from ill-health on 4 February 1970

RIGHT Flt Lt 'Pat' Lardner-Burke's personal markings of 53 years ago have been faithfully reapplied to MH434 following the fighter's first ever restoration, undertaken by John Romain's Aircraft Restoration Company at Duxford in 1994/95

RIGHT Although owned by Christopher Horsley, PR XI PL965 is hangared and maintained by the OFMC, and is regularly seen performing at airshows, and in film and TV work, alongside MH434. Flying the latter on this occasion is Ray Hanna, legendary ex-leader of the Red Arrows, and one of the world's most experienced single-seat pilots, with over 17,000 flying hours in his logbook. Formating with him is his son Mark, an equally seasoned Spitfire operator, and ex-RAF fighter pilot

BELOW Looking in better condition than when it was at the 'cutting edge' of Fighter Command in the late summer of 1943, the recently restored MH434 climbs out from Duxford with 110° of bank applied by pilot Mark Hanna in early 1995. The asymmetric radiators (combined coolant and intercoolant radiator on the right, and oil-cooler/coolant radiator on the left) under the wings were one of the main visual recognition features of the Mk IX, which looked very similar to a late-production Mk V when viewed from certain angles

R
ZD
B
MH434

RIGHT MH434 spent its entire frontline career flying with the Hornchurch Wing, seeing service with Nos 349 and 350 'Belgian' Sqns, as well as the 'Natal' Squadron. By mid-1944 the advent of newer spec Mk IXs, Packard-powered MK XVIs and the awesome Griffon-Spitfires meant that the fighter's brief frontline career was all but over, and it was duly put in store with No 9 MU at Cosford in March 1945, before transferring to No 76 MU at Wroughton for disposal.

Unlike many other combat veterans, MH434 beat the scrap man by being sold to the Royal Netherlands Air Force in early 1947 – they had it shipped straight from Tilbury to Batavia, in the Dutch East Indies. Here it saw action with No 322 Sqn against Nationalist forces struggling for independence – a total of 165 sorties were flown by MH434 in-theatre. Following a belly landing in 1949, the aircraft was returned to Holland, refurbished by Fokker, and sold to the Belgian Air Force.

After service with the *Ecole Pilotage Avance* and No 13 Wing, it was sold into civilian hands for use as a target tug in March 1956. It remained in this role, flying from Ostend, until 1963, when it was bought by Tim Davies, and flown back to Britain. Based at Elstree, the fighter was thoroughly overhauled, which included the refitting of its elliptical wingtips to decrease its stalling speed by five knots – this made it more manageable when flying in the tight confines of Elstree airfield.

MH434 was acquired by Spitfire Productions Ltd for the filming of *The Battle of Britain* in November 1967 (this was not the fighter's screen debut, however, as it had made a cameo appearance in MGM's *Operation Crossbow* in 1965), after which it was sold to Adrian Swire. It remained a firm airshow favourite throughout the 1970s, being duly recognised as one of the UK's first privately-owned 'warbirds'. In April 1983 it was sold at the famous Christie's auction at Duxford to Nalfire Aviation Ltd, a consortium led by Ray Hanna. MH434 has remained in his hands ever since, becoming one of the most cherished aircraft on the burgeoning airshow circuit

ZD
B
MH434
ELECTRICAL &
RADIO SOCKET

"Baby Bea V"
EXIT
NOT TO BE WALKED ON
WALKWAY FORWARD

RIGHT AND PREVIOUS PAGES Dutch Spitfire Flight LF IXC MK732 is another fighter with a combat pedigree, having flown sweeps over the D-Day beaches with No 485 Sqn, RNZAF, from Selsey. A one squadron machine, MK732 had been built at Castle Bromwich earlier in 1944, arriving at the frontline on 25 April. Assigned to Plt Off H W B Patterson (who christened the Spitfire *Baby Bea V* after his fiancee Beatrice), it was credited with a quarter-share in the destruction of a Ju 88 over the beach-head late in the afternoon of 6 June, its pilot on this occasion being Flt Lt K J Mac-donald. After participating in the Battle of Arnhem, MK732 was stored at Colerne. Here its sat for almost four years, until bought by the Royal Netherlands Air Force in June 1948. The Spitfire was coded H-25 and tasked with training Dutch fighter pilots, a role it undertook until being SoC in June 1954. Dan Griffith is at the controls here

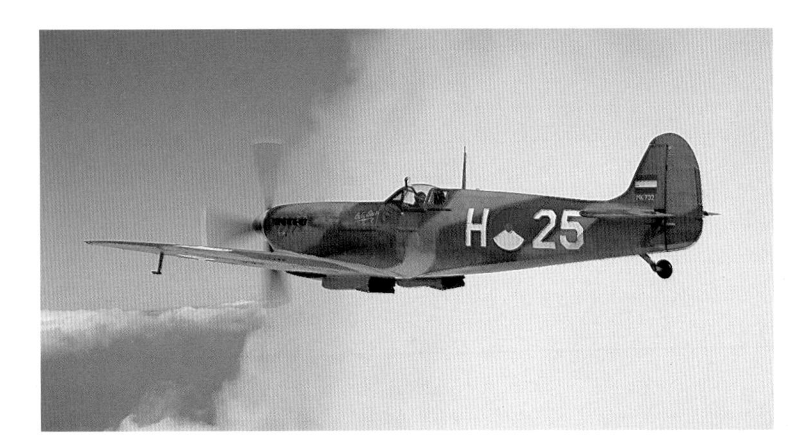

ABOVE MK732 spent a short while as a decoy at Eindhoven AFB, before being 'souvenired' by No 14 Sqn, RAF, and displayed outside the Officers' Mess at Gutersloh. It returned to the UK in 1969, where it was eventually issued to the BBMF for parts reclamation to allow its Spitfires to remain airworthy – its wing internals were used as patterns in the rebuild of damaged Mk V AB910 in the late 1970s

RIGHT AND BELOW The hulk of MK732 was returned to Holland for restoration in 1985, where a team led by Jack Van Egmond and Steve Atkins rebuilt the historic fighter using much of its original airframe. The Spitfire came back to England (Lydd airport) for final assembly in March 1993, prior to it taking to the skies for the first time three months later on 10 June

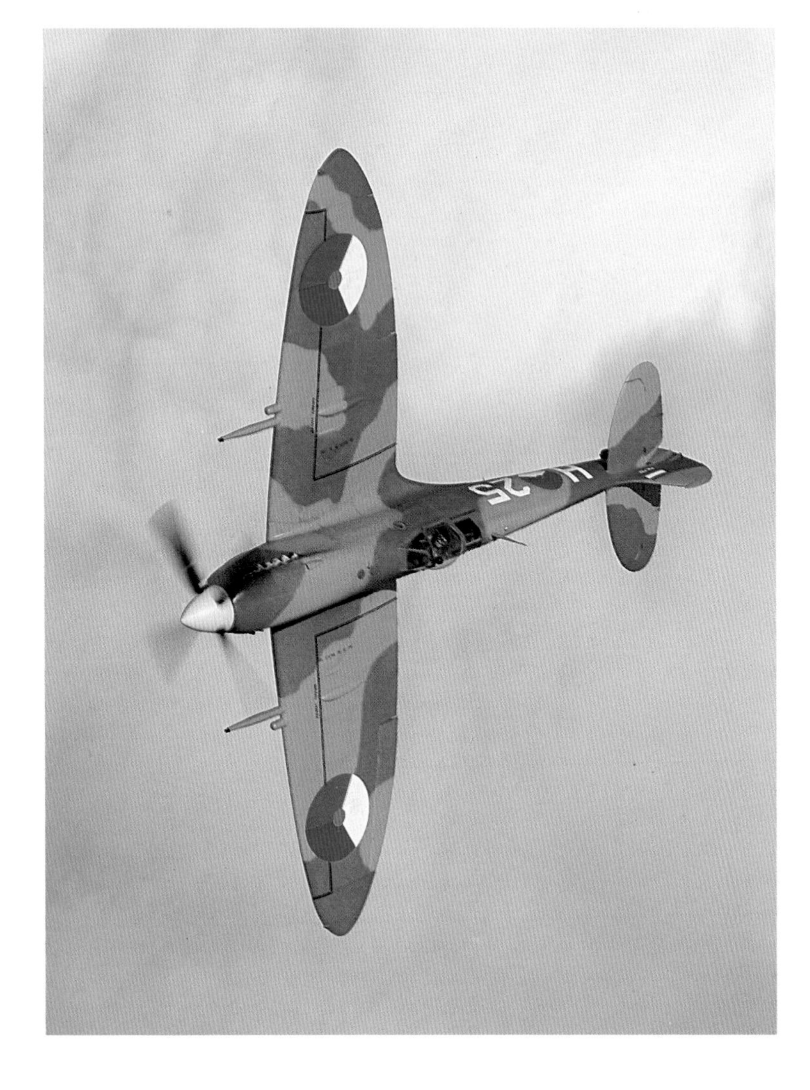

"Baby Bea V"
H 25
MK 732

LEFT Fighting over the same beaches as MK732 on D-Day was clipped wing Spitfire LF IXE ML417, which has flown in its period No 443 'Hornet' Sqn, RCAF, scheme ever since its restoration to airworthiness by Personal Plane Services at Booker for The Fighter Collection in the early 1980s. It is seen here at the latter's Duxford home following its participation in a summer display in 1991

RIGHT Nick Grey leans forward in his straps and peers through the windscreen in order to keep the T-6 photo-ship firmly in his sights whilst closely formating over Cambridgeshire farmland in the summer of 1993. His mount is a true combat veteran, being credited with the destruction of two Bf 109Gs over Arnhem on 29 September 1944, plus a Bf 109G and a Fw 190 damaged over Alencon and Falaise respectively in the first two weeks of July. ML417 didn't have things it own way all the time, however, being damaged by flak twice and mauled by a Bf 109G in the action over Arnhem

BELOW Looking remarkably like the Dover coast, ML417 cruises over the Normandy cliffs in June 1994, having been flown by Stephen Grey across the Channel in order to take part in the 50th anniversary of the D-Day landings. Soon after the real invasion had taken place five decades earlier, No 443 Sqn moved to St Croix Sur-Mer, with ML417 being one of the first Allied aircraft to land in France as part of 'Johnnie' Johnson's Canadian Wing. In the thick of the action for the next three months, ML417 finally parted company with the 'Hornet' Squadron when it was damaged over Holland. Its Canadian connection continued, however, after it was repaired, the fighter being sent to No 442 Sqn, which was part of the No 126 Canadian Wing, based in Belgium

ABOVE ML417 leads The Fighter Collection's Spitfire F XIVC MV293 and P-51D-25-NA Mustang 44-73149 along the Normandy coast behind B-25D-30-NC 43-3318 on the D-Day 50th anniversary weekend in 1994. The aircraft all recovered at Caen airport, where ML417 was graced with the presence of legendary ace 'Johnnie' Johnson, who had flown Mk IXs over the D-Day beaches

LEFT As the remnants of the Mulberry Harbour off the beach at Arromanches (*Gold* beach) disappear in the background, ML417 leads the Fighter Collection's five-ship formation east towards the *Juno* invasion beach. Joining the two Spitfires and the Mustang are P-47M Thunderbolt 45-19192 and a General Motors FM-2 Wildcat, both resplendent in full invasion stripes – ML417 is, however, the only true D-Day veteran in this formation.

Following its assignment to No 442 Sqn, the Spitfire was routinely swapped amongst the three Canadian Wing units, pilots from Nos 401 and 441 Sqns also using it in combat. After fighting its way east into Germany, ML417 ended its frontline service in the spring of 1945, serving briefly with Nos 412 and 411 Sqns, prior to both units re-equipping with Mk XVIs. Like many redundant Mk IXs, it was flown to High Ercall for storage in August 1945, and there it stayed until sold to Vickers Armstrongs on 31 October 1946 for conversion into a two-seat trainer for the Indian Air Force

THIS SPREAD ML417's Far Eastern sojourn remains shrouded in mystery, the aircraft finally ending up in the Indian Air Force Museum compound at Palam in 1967. There it remained until presented to US Senator Norman E Gaar in April 1971, who had it shipped to America the following year. It was sent to Darrell Skurich in Fort Collins, Colorado, for restoration, but little work was undertaken and the airframe was acquired by Stephen Grey in 1980. Shipped to PPS at Booker, ML417 was restored back to LF IXE specs by Joe Austin and Lawrence Laveris in just under three years.

Its first flight took place at Booker on 10 February 1984, and in June of that year it participated in the 40th anniversary flypasts over Normandy – a decade later it returned once again

LEFT Both restored by Historic Flying Ltd at Audley End, in Essex, LF IXE TE566 and LF XVIE RW382 (flown by Tim Routsis) hold formation beneath the 'photo-ship' on a sortie over Cambridgeshire in 1994. Although built as a clipped-wing Spitfire at Castle Bromwich in mid-1945, and flown in this configuration by the Czech Air Force, TE566 now flies with its elliptical tips in place as it improves the aircraft's stalling speed, and general handling characteristics, in the circuit

RIGHT AND BELOW Owned by The Historic Aircraft Collection of Jersey, TE566 was one of the last of 5665 Mk IXs built, and as such benefited from having a pointed Mk VII/VIII fin tip, 'E' wing (comprising two 20 mm cannon and two .5 in Browning machine guns) and the Merlin 68A engine. The machine was delivered to No 312 'Czech' Sqn at Manston in June 1945 as one of 72 Spitfires bought by the Czech government from Britain with a special £5 million loan organised between the two allies.

TE566 is being flown in this sequence by Charlie Brown

ABOVE AND RIGHT TE566 has been restored in the original scheme applied to all 72 Czech Spitfires at Manston prior to their departure for Prague-Ruzynet airport on 7 August 1945. Coded 'DU-A', denoting that it was Sqn Ldr H Hrbacek's aircraft, and wearing No 312 Sqn's stork emblem on its cowlings, the fighter was issued to the 2nd Division of the 4th and 5th Fighter Regiments at Ceské Budejovice soon after its arrival in Czechoslovakia. Redesignated S-89s (S for *Stihaci*, 'fighter' in Czech), the surviving Spitfires were finally relegated to the training role in 1947, before being sold to Israel the following year.

An initial batch of 50 Spitfires was sent to the Middle East in late 1948, with TE566 being amongst their number. Sadly, little is known of its subsequent career with the Israeli Air Force, other than it served with No 101 Sqn coded 20-32. Retired from service sometime in the mid-1950s, TE566 was 'put out to pasture' in the playground of a *Kibbutz* at Alonhim, from where it was retrieved in 1976 by 'warbird entrepreneur' Robs Lamplough. It remained in storage in a hangar at Duxford for the next six years until acquired by Guy Black's Aero Vintage Ltd, who moved it to their Sussex premises and commenced restoration alongside LF IX MJ730, also an ex-Israeli machine

RIGHT The team in Sussex made steady progress on the fighter before selling it to the Historic Aircraft Collection (HAC) of Jersey in 1986 – Guy Black continued managing the restoration despite this change of ownership. HAC moved TE566 to Hull Aero at Ludham, in Norfolk, where its badly damaged wings and tail unit were rebuilt – a job not completed until early 1989 owing to the lack of a substantial number of key parts. At the same time as this was taking place, its engine was being overhauled by Jersey Aviation, and by the end of 1990 all the various parts of the TE566 'puzzle' were ready for final assembly.

At this point it was decided by HAC to entrust the task of completing the rebuild to the seasoned Spitfire team at Historic Flying Ltd, and the aircraft was duly trucked to Audley End in early 1991. Here, the engine was mated with the fuselage and the myriad electrical, fuel and hydraulic lines connected up and test run. TE566's distinctive Czech scheme was also applied by the company, and finally on 2 June 1992 the fighter was test flown by Air Marshal Sir John Allison, some 16 years after it had been retrieved from Israel.

In this atmospheric shot Charlie Brown in TE566 formates with Tim Routsis in RW382 at sunset over Duxford

ABOVE AND RIGHT With so few Spitfires surviving the scrapper's torch after the war, it seems unbelievable that two former squadronmates could commemorate the 50th anniversary of D-Day in 1994 by performing a series of flypasts across England. MK732, featured earlier in this chapter, donned invasion stripes, RAF roundels and No 485 Sqn codes specially for the event, and joined up with Tr 9 ML407 (formerly an LF IXC) five decades after they had served together.

The latter enjoyed notable success over Normandy on D-Day afternoon when its Kiwi pilot, six-kill ace Flg Off 'Johnnie' Houlton, DFC, destroyed a Ju 88 south of Omaha Beach (this was the first Allied kill of the invasion) and shared in the destruction of a second Junkers. Later in the month Houlton used ML407 to destroy two Bf 109Gs, plus damage a third.

By 28 December 1944 ML407 had completed 137 sorties with No 485 Sqn, and was then reassigned to No 145 Wing of the 2nd TAF. From 28 December until VE-Day, ML407 saw action with a further seven units (including No 485 Sqn again), before finally being returned to the UK in mid-April 1945

RIGHT Having been in the frontline for just over a year, ML407 was returned to the UK and placed in storage, until being sold to Vickers Armstrongs in 1950

Converted to Tr 9 specs, it was acquired by the Irish Air Corps and operated until 1960. Brought back to England in 1968 as a 'spare' airframe for *The Battle of Britain* film, ML407 was bought by Nick Grace in August 1979, who set about meticulously restoring it at St Merryn, in Cornwall, over the next five years. ML407 took the skies once again on 16 April 1985, with its owner at the controls. Retain-ing its two-seater configuration, the fighter was repainted in its D-Day scheme, as seen in these shots.

Tragically, Nick Grace was killed in a car crash in October 1988, but his widow, Carolyn Grace (also an accomplished pilot), vowed to keep the Spitfire 'in the family', and soon decided to go one step further by learning to fly the fighter. Under the tutelage of seasoned pilot Peter Kynsey, Carolyn went solo on ML407 on 17 July 1990 after just four-and-a-half hours of dual instruction, thus making her the only female owner/operator of a Spitfire in the world. She is flying ML407 in this sequence of shots

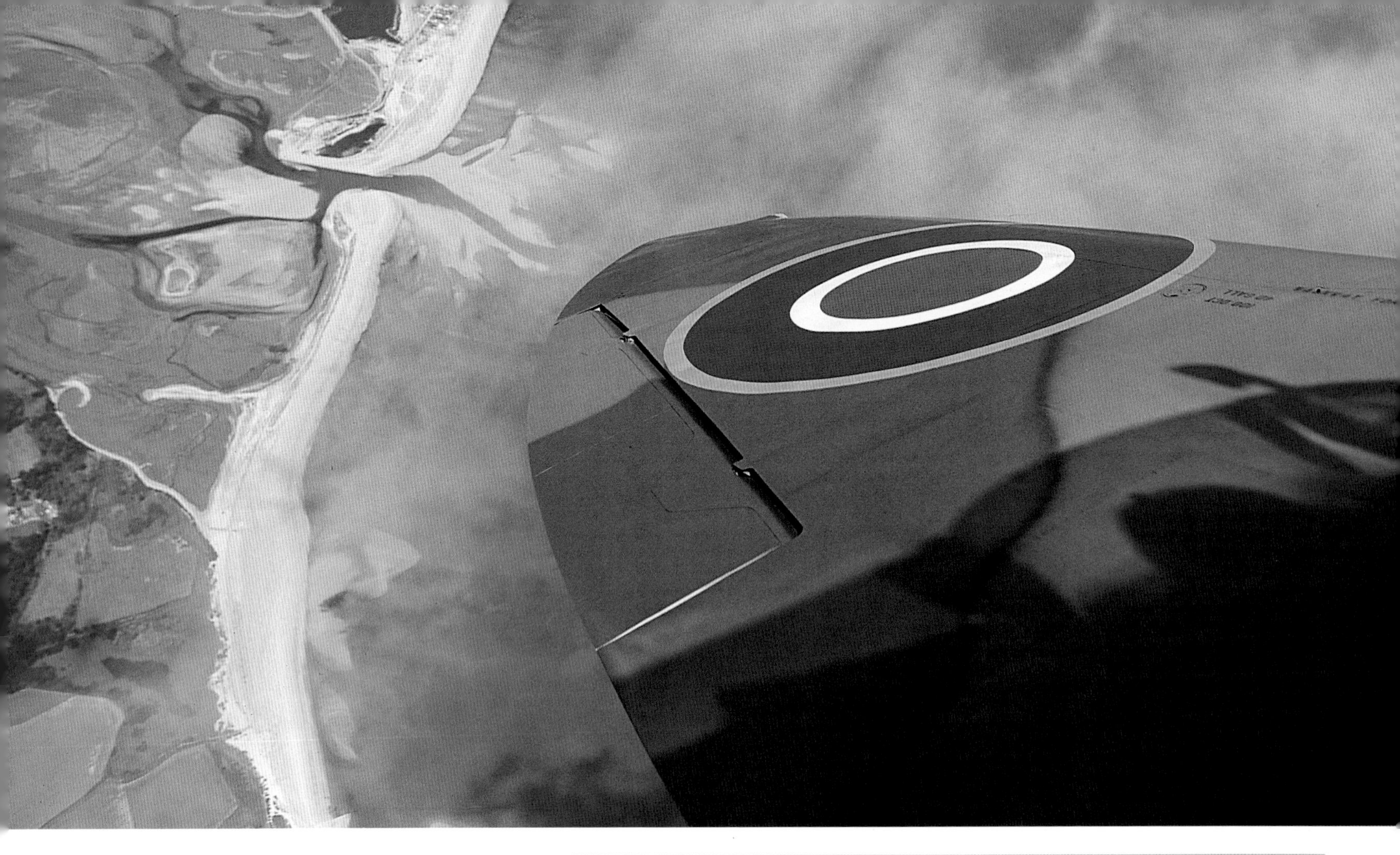

ABOVE On patrol over Portland, pilot Rick Roberts' head is silhouetted against the wing of his Spitfire, PV202

RIGHT Standing the aircraft on its tail, Rick Roberts opens up the Packard-Merlin 266 and climbs vertically in Tr 9 PV202. As with Carolyn Grace's two-seater, this machine was built as an LF IX at the Castle Bromwich works in 1944, although due to its later completion date it didn't arrive at the frontline (at the former Luftwaffe fighter base at Merville, in northern France) until October of that year. It was used in the close-support role by No 33 Sqn until the unit returned to the UK in mid-December to convert onto Tempests. PV202 also returned to England also, having flown 20 combat sorties whilst on the continent.

After a brief spell with a support unit, it was issued to No 412 'Falcon' Sqn at Heesch, in Holland, where it served alongside ML417. By the time the unit returned to the UK at the end of May 1945, PV202 had flown a further 76 operational sorties, and been credited with the destruction of two Fw 190s and one Bf 109G – kills shared between Flt Lt Joe Richards and Sqn Ldr 'Dewy' Dewan, both of No 412 Sqn.

Placed in storage at High Ercall, the forgotten warrior sat dormant until it was picked as one of the six airframes to be converted into Tr 9 specs (like ML407) for the Irish Air Corps in 1950. Like ML407, PV202 was retired at Baldonnel in December 1960, and returned to the UK in March 1968 when bought by N A W Samuelson

LEFT With the throttle retarded and the stick pushed forward, Rick Roberts dives down towards the Dorset coast, its authentic No 412 Sqn markings gleaming in the summer sun

VZ

INSET AND LEFT
After four years in storage PV202 was acquired by Sir William Roberts for his Strathallan collection. It was sold to Nick Grace along with ML407 in 1979, but the latter then agreed to pass PV202 onto Steve Atkins, who had also attempted to buy it from Sir William. Thus began the saga of PV202's restoration to airworthiness, which finally culminated in a successful 30-minute test flight by Peter Kynsey from Dunsfold on 23 February 1990. Ownership then passed to Richard Parker, who in turn sold PV202 onto Goodwood-based Rick Roberts

CHAPTER FIVE

SPITFIRE IN BLUE

Spitfire PR XI PL965

Flight Lieutenant H J S 'Jimmy' Taylor
No 16 Sqn
August to November 1944

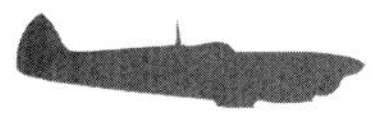

'Flying Photo-Recce (PR) sorties was regarded by many pilots, and especially by those fortunate enough to actually do it, as a "plum" job in the wartime RAF. To sit behind a throbbing Merlin 70 engine, powering a waxed and polished blue Spitfire PR XI, its wings stripped of guns and ammunition but holding extra gallons of petrol in the leading-edges, as it flew at 360 mph to a target hundreds of miles into enemy airspace to take urgently-needed photographs and, avoiding hostile flak and fighter interception, to return with them to base – this was the stuff of many a young pilot's dreams 51 years ago.

'The Spitfire PR XI, of which PL965 is one of only two examples still flying in the world, was the photo-recce version of the Spitfire Mk IX. It had an 85-gallon fuel tank in front of the pilot and 65 gallons in the leading-edge of each wing. With this fuel load, it had a duration of over five hours and a range of about 1500 miles. It carried a pair of F52 cameras, fitted with 36-in focal-length lenses, pointing down vertically through holes in the fuselage, with a side-by-side overlap of 10°. They were operated electrically and heated from the engine, and had magazines holding 500 exposures of roll-film, producing 8-in x 7-in prints. These gave a scale of 1:10,000 at 30,000 ft, and enabled quite small objects such as a man on a bicycle to be detected stereoscopically by the photographic interpreters, provided the prints overlapped fore-and-aft by 60 per cent.

'An F24 camera with a 14-in lens could be fitted in the fuselage behind the pilot's head to take oblique photographs at relatively low level – it was aimed by lining-up a mark on the canopy with a stripe on the port wing-tip. For low-level verticals, an F24 camera with 5-in lens could be fitted under each wing, pointing out at a slight angle and housed in a glazed protrusion. This was the equipment carried by

BELOW The No 16 Sqn pilot threads EN654 through the clouds as he climbs to cruising altitude soon after departing Northolt in October 1944. This particular PR XI was one of the first of its type issued to the unit, and as such is fitted with the rounded fin tip associated with contemporary Mk IXs of the period. It served two tours with No 16 Sqn, and in June 1945 was converted into a high-speed mail carrier. EN654 was SoC in 1947

ABOVE 'Jimmy' Taylor poses in 'his' Harvard at Upavon in December 1945

Spitfire PR XI PL965 to perform its photo-recce duties.

'The original objectives of PR had been mainly strategic – to gather intelligence about the German war-machine through regular photographic observation. When the time came to liberate Europe, however, 2nd Tactical Air Force was formed to operate with the Allied armies, and No 16 Sqn (formerly an Army Co-operation unit) became part of No 34 Wing to provide Montgomery's 21st Army Group with photographic reconnaissance beyond the range of its tactical recce squadrons. This involved taking photos of the targets selected for the Allied light bomber force – transport and communications centres, airfields, bridges, ammunition dumps, etc. – and a great deal of mapping of the terrain the infantry were going to have to fight over, especially the rivers, canals, roads and railways.

'We were also tasked quite often with strategic targets such as the Ruhr factories and the docks of Bremen, which were more easily reached from France and Belgium. When V1s and V2s began their assault on Britain and Belgium, it became a top priority for us to try to detect and photograph their elusive launch-sites.

'When I joined No 16 Sqn in August 1944 it was operating from RAF Northolt, but it soon moved to Normandy, then to Amiens, Brussels and finally Eindhoven, usually occupying airstrips or airfields recently vacated by Typhoon squadrons.

'The actual operational procedures of PR work were remarkably simple, being little different in basic outline from those practised by the heroic pilots and observers in flimsy two-seater biplanes during World War 1 – that is to say, our tools for getting to the target and back were maps, a compass and a stopwatch.

PR Individualists

'All sorties were flown alone, which perhaps explains why the unit was more a collection of individuals than a cohesive body of mutually supportive pilots, as were most bomber and fighter squadrons. The pilots' names were on a roster and the one at the top was given the next mission. The target, or series of targets, was explained to us in the Wing operations room by one of the Army or RAF Intelligence Officers and we marked it on our maps with blue wax crayon. We then went to the Met office to get the wind strength and direction and the weather at the target and en route to it.

'We returned to our No 16 Sqn operations room (which was little more than a large caravan with canvas extensions to each side), drew our track-lines on the map, worked out our courses from a triangle of velocities on our Dalton calculator, and marked-in 10-minute or 20-mile way-stages along our track. We would jot down the significant features and our ETA at them on our knee-pad. We would also decide the direction for our photo runs, upwind and downwind, and work out the time-interval between exposures to give us the necessary 60 per cent overlap. For example, if we expected a 100-mph wind at 30,000 ft, this would give us a ground-speed of 460 mph downwind, but only 260 mph upwind. The exposure interval might be six seconds downwind, but ten seconds on our slower course upwind. We had to set this exposure interval on our camera control-box just before we started our photo run. We hoped sincerely that Met's forecast winds were right, as we had no means of checking them once we had taken off.

'In No 16 Sqn we did not have our own personal aircraft and groundcrew. The Engineering Officer would have been given details of our sortie, and he in turn would have selected the next available Spitfire and had it fitted with the correct cameras and lenses. Take-off would be timed for the best Met conditions, and we would go out to the aircraft with the mechanic standing by and inspect it carefully. He would then help to strap us into the cockpit and give the windscreen a final polish once the machine had

been given the all-clear by the pilot. After starting the engine on the external batteries on a trolley, we would check the systems very thoroughly, especially the blind-flying instruments, the oxygen, the radio on the various frequencies, the electrics, the oil pressure, the radiator cooling, and the compressed air pressure – failure of any of these would mean changing to another aircraft.

'After a final run-up to check the magnetos, the constant-speed pitch-control of the propeller, and the power output at full-throttle, we would wave "chocks away" and taxy out quickly to the runway – the coolant would boil if we stayed on the ground too long. A green light from airfield control, a beautiful surge of power from the engine, and we would be off. I usually climbed up in a wide circle and set course from the centre of the airfield.

'The flight would now become interesting. In the autumn of 1944, the weather over northern Europe was generally overcast - and we could not take photographs through cloud. Our targets were given to us on the days when Met predicted that the cloud-cover over the target would be five-tenths or less; sometimes we were told this even though on the airfield it was totally overcast and raining. So we might well find ourselves going into cloud and flying by instruments a few minutes after take-off, breaking out into clear air at 20,000 ft or so.

'Our planned operational height was 30,000 ft, but the actual height was governed by the altitude at which our exhaust gases condensed out to form a white "contrail" behind us, giving the Germans ample evidence of our presence even though the blue Spitfire itself was invisible at this height. Contrails usually occurred at 24,000 to 27,000 ft, so we flew either above or below that level, using our rear-view mirror to check that we were not leaving a trail.

'On a clear day, high-level navigation was not too difficult, as we had plenty of time to read our maps and distinguish landmarks on the ground. But if the gaps in the clouds predicted by Met did not materialise, we had to come down through the clouds until we emerged into the relative gloom below them. It was here that all our careful course-plotting would bear fruit – or not. Spiralling down through 15,000 ft of cloud would upset all our calculations of time

ABOVE The pilot looks on as a member of his groundcrew carefully squeezes the F24 oblique camera into its hatch behind the cockpit. Clearly staged for the benefit of the press photographer, this routine was usually completed well before the pilot arrived to 'sign' for his aircraft prior to take-off. Again, a quick check of the Spitfire's fin tip reveals that this anonymous machine is an early-production PR XI

and distance, and it was much more difficult to distinguish landmarks at a lower level.

'Taking a series of overlapping pictures over a stretch of canal or railway, or in mapping a certain area, was bedevilled by the fact that we could only see beneath us, to check that we had not drifted off the target, by turning the Spitfire on its side and looking down through the canopy. This had to be done in the short interval between exposures, but it upset both our gyro compass and our liquid-bowl one, so it was difficult to come back onto our original heading. I often felt that successful photography under these conditions was more a matter of luck than good judgement!

'All the time we were airborne, we could hear the German radar whining in our ear-phones and knew that we were under observation. We felt we could out-fly and out-run the usual enemy fighters, but the German jets were just coming into operation, and because they were always vastly outnumbered by Allied fighters, they regarded the solitary high-flying spy-planes as fair game. But their duration was short and we reckoned we could out-manoeuvre them until they had to go home. I had one such encounter with a then-unidentified Arado Ar 234, which chased me up to 39,000 ft, but did not open fire. Perhaps he was on a training flight, or possibly also a photo recce sortie.

'No 16 Sqn suffered many casualties (nine pilots failed to return between August 1944 and the end of the war) and the possible causes were very diverse – fighter interception, flak, oxygen, instrument or engine failure, navigation error. Some are known, but some still remain a mystery (Taylor himself suffered engine failure in PR XI MB957 over Holland on 19 November 1944 whilst on a photo-recce sortie over airfields in Germany, Ed.). But our morale was always very high, largely because of the enormous respect we had for our CO, Sqn Ldr Tony Davis, DFC, a veteran of 26, who always took the most dangerous missions for himself. We also had infinite trust in our sturdy Spitfires, and PL965, which served with the unit between January and September 1945, is both a remarkable survivor and reminder of those unforgettable days.'

BELOW Heavy autumn rains in October 1944 turned Eindhoven airfield into a lake for a number of weeks, and pilots had to be careful not to nose over as they were taxying from their dispersals to the main runway. PL883 served with No 400 'City of Toronto' Sqn for much of 1944/45, and survived the war to see service with the Royal Danish Air Force in the late 1940s

ABOVE Its twin F52 vertical camera ports just visible beneath the fuselage roundel, PL965 (with Mark Hanna at the controls) banks away from the photo-ship. Other distinguishing features of the PR XI include the deepened nose contour, which houses an enlarged oil tank, and a retractable tailwheel like the Spitfire MK VII/VIII

TOP RIGHT Performing only his second ever Spitfire flight, No 19 Sqn's Andy Gent formates with the photo-ship over Cambridgeshire on 27 October 1995.

Built at Aldermaston in September 1944 as one of 471 PR XIs constructed by Supermarines, PL965 waited until 11 January 1945 before it was issued to No 16 Sqn

RIGHT PL965 saw much action with the unit, performing 40 sorties over western Germany in advance of the Allied armies as they pushed further into the Reich – indeed, on 21 March 1945 the PR XI flew no less than four trips in one day. PL965 remained in Holland after VE-Day, finally returning to the UK to be placed in storage in late 1945

PL965
R

PL965

FAR LEFT During 1994 PL965 was resprayed in a Fighter Command scheme and masqueraded as a Mk IX in order to undertake film work alongside the OFMC's MH434. The PR XI is seen here with Mark Hanna in the cockpit

ABOVE With shooting completed on various projects by the autumn of 1995, PL965 reverted to its more authentic overall PR Blue scheme and 'R' code, as worn during its No 16 Sqn days 50 years earlier. Although owned by Christopher Horsley, the PR XI is maintained and flown by the OFMC, sharing hangar space with MH434 at the company's Duxford facility. In this shot, Mark (in the foreground) and Ray Hanna take advantage of the unseasonably fine November weather to put both Spitfires through their paces, prior to 'putting them away' for winter

LEFT Detail views of two of PL965's unique features – namely the F24 oblique camera port and the deepened nose contours

B
R

LEFT PL965's spell in storage came to an end in July 1947 when it was one of eight Spitfires (two Mk XIVs, two Mk XVIs and four Mk XIs) bought for the rumoured sum of £25.00 each by the Royal Netherlands Air Force (RNAF) to serve as technical training aids. PL965 was issued to a school at Deelan upon its arrival in Holland.

By 1953 the Spitfire's career as a fighter with the RNAF was coming to a close, with the survivors of the 55 Mk IXs supplied to the Dutch seven years earlier being finally retired, which also meant that the instructional Spitfires were no longer required. Fortunately, someone with a sense of history eventually convinced the powers that be at Deelan that PL965 would make an ideal 'guardian' for the Sergeants' Mess, and so it was duly displayed in 1955, with certain cowling parts coming from the other 'static' Spitfires, which were all eventually scrapped

RIGHT In 1960 PL965 was sold to the National War and Resistance Museum at Overloon. Here it remained exposed to the elements for the next 27 years, although it was twice refurbished (by Harry van der Meer and Fred Vinju in 1973, and then three years later by a team at RAF Brüggen).

Finally, just when it appeared that spreading corrosion in the airframe would render this rare Spitfire fit for scrap only, it was swapped in 1987 by Nick Grace for Mk XIV NH649, and sent to the Medway Aircraft Preservation Society Ltd (MAPSL) at Rochester for rebuilding to airworthiness. Christopher Horsley took over ownership of the PR XI following Nick Grace's death in October 1988, and the aircraft finally flew, with Mark Hanna at the controls, on 23 December 1992 – some 45 years after its last flight!

R
PL965

CHAPTER SIX

GRIFFON SPITFIRE

Spitfire F Mk XIVEs SM832 and NH799, and F Mk XIVC MV293

Wing Commander Pete Brothers
Culmhead Wing
April to October 1944

'During deep penetration fighter sweeps over France in 1944 my three squadrons would spread out in pairs in a near line-abreast formation, thus allowing us to cover a vast swathe of sky. This formation comprised two squadrons equipped with Spitfire F VIIs and a solitary unit with Mk XIVs. Range was never a great problem, as both marks had an increased fuel capacity when compared with either the Mk V or IX, boasting extra tanks in the wings.

'Although the Mk VII was nicer to fly from a handling point of view, the Mk XIV was the real performer thanks to its Griffon engine. It was a truly impressive machine, being able to climb almost vertically – it gave many Luftwaffe fighter pilots the shock of their lives when, having thought that they had bounced you from a superior height, they were astonished to find the Mk XIV climbing up to tackle them head-on, throttle wide open! I would love to have had a whole wing of these aircraft.

'I was given command of the Culmhead Wing (originally known as the Exeter Wing) in April, and this consisted of No 610 Sqn with Spit XIVs, No 41 Sqn with Spit XIIs, Nos 616 and 131 Sqns with Spit VIIs, No 126 Sqn with Spit IXs and No 263 Sqn with Typhoons! They were scattered all over the place – No 41 Sqn was at Bolthead, Nos 126 and 263 Sqns at Harrowbeer, and the rest at Culmhead. This arrangement really was quite ridiculous, and I explained my case to No 10 Group Ops Officer, Grp Capt Tom Dalton-Morgan (who had earlier achieved notoriety as a Hurricane ace with No 43 Sqn in 1940/41, Ed.), telling him that every time I went to visit a squadron away from Culmhead I would be recalled half way there with the order that his office had ordered a wing sweep!

'This usually resulted in me rushing back to Culmhead just in time to see the wing departing, with me lacking sufficient fuel to join them. I therefore suggested to him that he form a second wing at Harrowbeer with the two Spit units and the single Typhoon squadron, which he duly did.

'I remained at Culmhead with a wing comprising Spit VIIs and XIVs, both of which boasted a superb range that allowed us to sweep as far east over the continent as the Swiss border. On these missions we hit anything that took our fancy – vehicles, trains and airfields, mostly. We would brief our missions based around a route worked out for us by Group, who would tell us that our sweep would act as a diversion for a larger formation of bombers hitting a target in the general vicinity. We would patrol over France at 6000 ft, in order to be above the light flak, and generally look out for trains and other targets.

BELOW Although the identity of the individual flying Spitfire F XIVC RB140 remains a mystery, a close inspection of the original print reveals a face that looks remarkably like that of the legendary Jeffrey Quill, then Vickers-Supermarine's Chief Test Pilot. This dates the shot as having been taken in the autumn of 1943, Quill flying this aircraft (the first production-standard Mk XIV built) in October of that year. He described it as 'a splendid and potent aeroplane', although he felt its longitudinal and directional characteristics still required work – these handling-problems caused by the Griffon engine's barely controllable levels of torque remained with the 'small fin' Mk XIV throughout its life.

RB140 went on to serve very briefly with No 616 Sqn in early 1944, before being adorned with the 'DW' codes of No 610 Sqn and operating in Pete Brothers' Culmhead Wing. It was irreparably damaged in combat over France on 30 October 1944

'On one of these sorties one of my pilots spotted a flak train steaming along below us. I acknowledged his call, but proceeded to fly along on the same course, thus giving the enemy the impression that we hadn't seen them. After flying on for a further 20 miles, I gave the order to drop down to the deck and turn back in towards the train. At that height all you could see was the smoke from the engine, and we waited until the train vanished into a thick wood before we lined up for our single attacking pass.

'We timed our approach perfectly, and as the engine emerged from the wood I squared it up in my gunsight and gave it a broadside of cannon. The other pilots followed suit, and by the time the deadly flak batteries had emerged from the wood we were on our way, having left the engine a hissing wreck.

V1 busting

'We also hit a fair number of *No Ball* V1 missile launch sites during this period, which were heavily defended by mobile AA batteries. As I was on my fourth tour I had convinced myself that I would not survive to see VE-Day. As a result of my state of mind, I would think nothing of handing over the lead of the wing to my Number Two, and diving down on a flak battery that had opened up on us as we flashed past at low-level. This was, in all honestly, a waste of ammunition as you rarely damaged the gun itself, and even if you did succeed in killing the crew, they were soon replaced – indeed, their chances of destroying an expensive aeroplane, and a trained pilot to boot, were far greater than your odds of knocking the battery out. I finally began to resist the temptation of strafing these targets after see colleagues lost to flak damage, but every now and then they would irritate me so much I just had to dive down and give them a squirt!

'The three-squadron wing itself was quite easy to control on a sweep as we generally spread out in pairs in virtually line abreast formation. The Spit VII was a favourite for these sweeps due to its range, although the XIV was the ultimate machine for this type of sortie. With the latter not only did you have the range, but it also boasted the performance to match – you could climb near vertically in the XIV and take on chaps diving down on you thinking they had

bounced you! It was simply a matter of turning into them, standing the aircraft on its tail and opening the throttle to climb up and engage the enemy.

'On 21 July 1944 we completed three trips in a day, and thinking that the action was over till the morrow as the sun was setting and the whole wing needed refuelling and rearming, we all adjourned to the mess for a meal, followed by a suitable spell in the bar after a hard day's work. The telephone rang late in the evening and it was Tom Dalton-Morgan, who instructed me to take the wing down to Manston that night in order to be ready for a big show early the following morning. I informed him that there was only myself and two of the squadron COs who had ever flown Spits at night on the wing, but that didn't seem to concern him unduly! We quickly downed our beer, went out to our aircraft and took off.

'When we arrived overhead at Manston I was astonished to see the airfield lit up like a Christmas tree. I initially gave the instruction to land from the back of the formation, thus getting all the junior chaps down first, but it soon became chaotic, with chaps overshooting and generally milling around in the rather crowded airspace over the station. With fuel running low I decided to land, and after a simple recovery, followed the green light of the "Follow Me Van" around the Peri track to the dispersal.

'Another aircraft duly came up alongside and parked whilst I undid my straps, the groundcrew having already leapt up onto the wings of my Spitfire and commenced refuelling. The cry of "Christ. Bring a torch somebody. Where are the ****ing filler caps?" from an airman attempting to repeat the refuelling process on the fighter next to me, made me turn my attention to the dark mass of metal barely 30 ft away. A torch duly arrived and to the airman's surprise, he found he was sitting on the wing of Bf 109G-6/U2 Wk-Nr 412951 – a nightfighter from I./JG 301 – with its pilot (a Lt Horst Prenzel, Ed.) still huddled in the cockpit! He had simply landed after me and followed "his" green light around to the dispersal area.

'All hell then broke loose, as the wingman of this mysterious visitor had also attempted to land, but less successfully, the German fighter having come to a halt with its undercarriage in tatters. Thinking it was a Spitfire that had come to grief, the station ambulance and fire tender sped out to the wreck, only to find a Bf 109 in the middle of the airfield, minus its pilot. A full-scale alert was sounded, and after much siren ringing and frantic searching, they finally found this poor chap hiding behind some packing cases in one of the hangars on the edge of the airfield!

'Their story was that they had launched out of Holland, shot down a Lancaster over the North Sea, and then turned around to head home. After crossing the Thames Estuary they thought they were home, and duly landed at the first airfield they had come across. The RAF Intelligence Officer didn't believe this for a minute, as the Luftwaffe never lit up their airfields like the Allies. He thought that the pilots had simply had enough of the war and decided to surrender, which was a good thing really as both fighters were fully armed and could have caused havoc amongst our overshooting, gear-dangling, Spitfires.

Sweep leader

'I tried to lead as many sweeps as I could. I would attach myself to a squadron and lead the unit on the sortie, with the squadron commander flying as my number two, or perhaps leading one of his flights. For the Manston mission, Tangmere Wing were going to sweep around west of Paris, out through Belgium and then back to base, while we were doing exactly the same thing a little bit later, but in the opposite direction, to pick up anything that had been scrambled. At about the same time the Hornchurch Wing were patrolling in the Brussels area, so in all over 150 RAF fighters would be airborne over the continent at about the same time. However, we never came across a single enemy aircraft either on the ground or in the air.

'At this time I had both a Spit VII and a XIV at my disposal, each marked up with my personal code letters, "PB". Although the latter machine was superior to all wartime marks of Spitfire that I operated, I usually flew the former on sweeps due to its longer legs and similarity with the bulk of the wing's aircraft.

'We also flew daylight bomber escort missions in our long-range Spits, with three-and-a-half-hour sortie becoming quite commonplace. Quite often, the hardest thing we faced on these endurance sorties was the dinghy we sat on, which become extremely uncomfortable after a while! On one particular raid, in which we had 250 Lancasters under our protection, I remember that my number two and I had taken the very tail of the formation, due to the fact that we thought it would be more fun back there.

'The remainder of my two squadrons were split into pairs on either side of the bomber stream from the mid way point back, whilst Wg Cdr "Birdy" Bird-Wilson (also a Hurricane ace from 1940 with No 17 Sqn, Ed.) had his Harrowbeer Wing spread over the front half of the formation. Just to emphasise how physically large our task was, whilst I was talking to "Birdy" on the R/T, he was passing over the Channel Islands and I was just leaving the suburbs of Bordeaux with the tail end of the column!

'We had one Lancaster who really was lagging miles behind the remainder of the force, and I kept going back to try and urge him on because he really was a sitting duck, but all the crew would do in response was wave back at me! We couldn't really leave the rest of the "heavies" unprotected, so I would spend most of my time patrolling up and down the formation, then quickly belting back to check on our errant Lancaster. Fortunately, the Luftwaffe wisely decided to leave us alone on all of these sorties, and we never lost a single bomber to fighter attacks.'

Flight Lieutenant Don Healey
No 17 Sqn
1944 to 1946

'We didn't get off to a great start with the Mk XIVE as the first one that arrived at Madura flew straight through the base flying control caravan, situated at the end of the runway, whilst landing. The ferry pilot got out unscathed, but the aircraft was a write-off, as was the empty caravan.

BELOW Seasoned Burma campaigner Flt Lt Don Healey sits in his 'YB'-coded Spitfire F XIVE at Madura, in India, in August 1945. Although No 17 Sqn had barely seen a month's worth of flying with their brand new aircraft, this photo reveals just how worn they soon looked (*Don Healey*)

'Sadly, our next three crashes with the Mk XIV each proved fatal, and occurred during our work-ups for the carrier deployment aboard HMS *Trumpeter* as part of Operation *Zipper* – the invasion of Malaya. An aircraft flown by Flt Sgt Harry Lee had collided with a high tension cable during low flying training in mid-July 1945, killing the pilot. A few days later on 19 July 1945 the Air Marshal Inspector General of the RAF journeyed to Madura in his Beech Expediter to see how we were coping with the new Spitfires, and our Sqn Ldr Lacey decided to impress him by having a quartet of Spitfires intercept the "twin" and escort him to base. This was completed successfully, and once on the ground and inspecting the troops, the four Spitfires began to perform a steep formation dive-bombing display, pulling out in line astern and then rolling upward back to altitude.

'Halfway through the first slow roll, number two in the formation, Flt Sgt "Titch" Gardener, had his aircraft break up around him, killing the pilot in the ensuing crash. Seconds later Flt Sgt "Mo" Whiting's machine did the self same thing, with equally fatal results – sadly, both pilots were close friends who had trained together at Thornhill, in Rhodesia. Flt Sgt "Dutch" Holland in the number four slot hit the wreckage of Whiting's Spitfire, but was able to recover at Madura in a high-speed landing – the increased velocity was caused by the absence of part of his port wing and aileron.

'The squadron was immediately grounded, and the ensuing investigation found that all of our aircraft had loose wings where the main spar was bolted onto the centre section. The spar was held in place on either side of the fuselage by 3/4-in bolts, which should have been refrigeration fitted. However, the aircraft had arrived in kit form by boat, and were then assembled by TATA Airways, in Karachi, without the aid of suitable refrigeration equipment. The company's airframe fitters had found that the only way to secure what they assumed were oversize bolts in the wing join assembly was to reduce their diameter with emery cloth! The rectification work later put in hand by our engineers to fix this gross error saw each and every spar hole reamed out to a larger size, and special bolts made to fit the resulting aperture – they tested out all right after this modification.

'We had originally been allocated bubble-canopy FR Mk XIVs, but when the first one arrived at Madura Sqn Ldr Lacey exclaimed that it "wasn't a bloody Spitfire". Despite our protestations concerning the unrivalled visibility out of the canopy, "Ginger" wouldn't budge, and they were passed to

No 11 Sqn, whose pilots were more than happy to receive them in place of their war-weary Hurricane IICs. Eventually we got our complement of high-back F XIVEs, which fortunately satisfied our boss.

Hairy Beast

'The Mk XIV was a hairy beast to fly, and took some getting used too. I personally preferred the old Mk V from a flying standpoint, but you talk to someone like Pete Brothers and he swears by the Griffon-engined Spitfire, whilst Jeffrey Quill reckoned that the Mk VIII was the best of the lot.

'We were fortunate enough to be based at Madura when we received our first Mk XIVs as the runway here was over 3000 yards long, and fully concreted. It had been an important base for RAF Liberator units bombing Burma and Malaya in 1944/45, and was ideally suited for a squadron coming to grips for the first time with the vicious torque swing of the Griffon engine.

'We were told to open the throttle very slowly at the start of our take-off, with full opposite rudder applied to offset the five-bladed prop, which was driven by the Griffon in the opposite direction to the Merlin – this took some getting used to! Even with full aileron, elevator and rudder, this brute of a fighter still took off slightly sideways! However, once you picked up flying speed, and trimmed the rudder and elevator, this torque pull became bearable.

'One aspect you always had to bear in mind with the Mk XIV that no flying surface trimming could allow for was its considerable weight – it tipped the scales at 8475 lbs when fuelled and armed, which made it over 2000 lbs heavier than the Mk VIII. Therefore, extra height had to be allowed for when rolling and looping, as it tended to "wash out" when being flown in this way. "Ginger" Lacey graphically showed us all just how serious a problem this was when he attempted to do a loop from what he thought was an adequate starting height over Madura one afternoon. At the bottom of the loop he cleared the ground by barely four feet, and upon recovering back at the field Lacey looked ten years older than when he took off. He immediately gathered us around and told us in no uncertain terms not to attempt a similar manoeuvre with anything less than a 4000-ft reading on the altimeter.

'Most of our work-up time at Madura was spent preparing for the carrier launch from *Trumpeter* as part of the occupation of Malaya. A dummy flight-deck had been painted on the long runway to assist us in working on the length of our launching runs, but despite countless attempts at reducing the length of our take-offs, the best we could do was to part company with the tarmac 100 yards beyond the white line which theoretically marked the bow of the carrier! After much head-scratching, and a few sleepless nights, a Navy batsman was sent down to Madura to advise us that we would have the benefit of a 16-knot wind over the deck, although our take-off run was still to be only 270 ft long.

'Fortunately, we did not have to fly the aircraft aboard the small escort carrier in the first place, the Mk XIVs being craned onto the deck. Nevertheless, we still had to take-off from the vessel, and the flight-deck was crammed full of Austers and Fairchilds, as well as our Spits. Once in the Straits of Malacca, our aircraft were arranged in three-abreast V-formation as far astern as they could be pushed. Rather stupidly, it was decided that we should launch first one at a

ABOVE RM972 and an anonymous F XIVE model No 17 Sqn's distinctive chain-mailed gauntlet (an emblem inspired by the unit's Gloster Gauntlets of the late 1930s), which was applied to all their Griffon Spitfires after VJ-Day. A number of the unit's Mk VIIIs had also worn this emblem during the final push into Burma earlier in 1945 (*Don Healey*)

BELOW A Flight's Flg Off Geoff Curtis keeps the throttle open and the stick firmly back in No 17 Sqn's RN205 as it roars off the bow of the escort carrier *Trumpeter* on 9 September 1945. Note the slightly split trailing edge flaps, prised open with wedges of wood inserted specially for this one-off launch (*Don Healey*)

time, rather than the much more nimble Army AOP machines, so a good third of the deck was covered astern with these machines!

'Our groundcrews had trimmed the brake drums on the undercarriage until they were almost binding, and removed the wire "gate" from the throttle, which when combined allowed us to open the Griffon up to nearly full boost without the fighter running off down the deck. We had practised back at Madura in this configuration, and with the brake lever fully on, the throttle well open, the stick pulled back into the pit of your stomach and opposite rudder applied to offset the prop torque, you could actually get the aircraft to lift its tail off the ground and still remain stationary – but only for a matter of seconds! Once you felt the brakes slip you released the lever, banged the trottle through the gate and shot off down the deck.

'Dive-bomber'

'One final mod made by the groundcrews came into play once you were accelerating down the deck – small wooden blocks shaped into a 23° wedge were made to fit in between the wing and the flaps when in the closed position, as the latter could not be partially deployed for the launch. They pushed the flaps open about two inches, and gave the aircraft just a touch more lift. We had great fun flying back over the carrier after take-off and flipping the flap lever into the open position, which of course left the blocks to freefall back onto the deck of the ship – the Navy weren't at all pleased about being dive-bombed by their former guests!

'Despite using virtually all 2000+ hp from the aircraft's Griffon 65 engine, the bow of the ship still looked like it was perched just under the fighter's bulbous nose, and I was convinced I was never going to take-off before I ran out of steel deck. I had my parachute harness undone, shoulder straps loosened and the cockpit entry door ajar at the back, which stopped the canopy from travelling down its runners and inadvertently closing should you have to ditch straight after take-off – all other squadron pilots followed suit. Flying helmets weren't buckled up, and the intercom microphone lead was left out of its socket, being rolled up and tucked in your breast pocket. This way neither item could catch on something and foul your exit from the cockpit.

'We had been briefed not to immediately vacate our Spitfires should we crash into the sea off the end of the carrier, as invariably the vessel would ride over you and churn you up in its wake. It was suggested that we hold our breath, sink with the Spitfire, and then swim to the surface once the carrier had passed overhead – I wasn't too keen on this idea! As it transpired, all of us got off the *Trumpeter* without any snags or great dramas.

'After flying the short distance east over the Straits of Malacca to Kelanang, we landed to find the runway lined with abandoned Japanese Army fighters, bombers and trainers, all of which had been allocated for *kamikaze* missions against the Allied invasion fleet – thank God for VJ-Day.'

Flight Lieutenant Ron Hitchcock
No 26 Sqn
June 1945 to February 1946

'I joined the RAF in February 1940, promising my parents that I would not become a pilot – they were far from keen to see me earn my wings – so I became an apprentice instruments repairer. My first posting after the completion of my training was to a maintenance unit in Lincolnshire, where I spent my time travelling around the county picking up "dead" aircraft. I soon became bored of this, and fortunately was posted overseas in December 1940. I finished up in Singapore assigned as an "instrument basher", come stand-in rear air gunner, to No 36 Sqn, who were equipped with the inelegant Vickers Vildebeest III (a type the squadron had flown from Seletar since July 1935, Ed.).

BELOW Flt Lt Ron Hitchcock poses alongside 'his' Spitfire FR XIVE whilst with No 26 Sqn at Lübeck in August 1945. The oblique camera port in the starboard side of the aircraft is clearly visible in this photograph. Although 'Ginger' Lacey thought the 'bubble top' Spitfire destroyed the aircraft's classic lines, and thus refused to allow his unit to operate them, on the other side of the world the one-piece Perspex canopy was welcomed by photo-recce pilots charged with patrolling the still tense border areas of a recently-occupied Germany in the autumn of 1945 (*Ron Hitchcock*)

'After five months in the Far East, the RAF asked for volunteers to learn to fly, and I felt that I would miss the whole war if I stayed stuck out here, so I broke my promise and applied! Things took a turn for the worst come 1942 when the Japanese poured into Malaya from the north. I was with the squadron on the east coast of the country at Kuantan at the time, and scuttled back south to Singapore rather sharpishly, only to find that I had been posted on a pilots' course, along with 23 others!

'We managed to get out on a refugee ship to India, and then on to South Africa and up to Rhodesia, where I was the only one out of the two-dozen that left Singapore to gain my wings – and a commission. I returned to England in April 1943, only to be told that the RAF had a surplus of pilots. I was given the option of doing a ground tour, or going on an instructor's course – I had done rather well in the basic training phase of my wings course, which marked me out as sound material to pass on my skills to new instructors.

'I thought that this posting would only last for 12 months, but of course I got stuck in Training Command and ended up doing 600 hours in Tiger Moths! I finally nagged my way out of this posting and was sent to an Advanced Flying Unit (AFU), where I learnt to fly Harvards and Master IIs, before progressing onto war-weary Hurricane IIs and Spitfire Mk Vs at Hawarden in November 1944.

'I finally arrived at No 26 Sqn in May 1945, the unit having just returned to Chilbolton from Cognac/Château Bernard. They had been posted back to the England in order to transition from Mustang Is to the Spitfire FR XIV, making them amongst the first units in the RAF to receive this advanced mark. The Army were particularly interested in our progress, and a number of senior officers came down to our base to see the recce-optimised Spits being put through their paces.

Army Co-operation

'I was almost exclusively involved with Army co-operation sorties in the FR XIV whilst with the unit. Of course, in the middle of our transition the war ended, which left me feeling rather frustrated to say the least – I had spent the entire conflict trying to see action, but never had! Indeed, of the three pilots that arrived with me at No 26 Sqn, none of the had seen frontline service either, but had literally thousands of hours flying as instructors on Harvards and Tiger Moths. The bulk of the remaining pilots on the unit were all Army captains who had previously flown Auster Co-op aircraft – our RAF quartet had more flying hours individually that the Army pilots put together!

'My hours of droning about in the instructional role paid dividends at No 26 Sqn as the FR XIV was quite a handful to fly, particularly after having learnt on Spitfire Mk IIs and Vs – the latter were quiet and beautifully balanced "flying machines", whilst the Griffon Spit was a loud and spirited machine on the wing. However, they all shared the mark trait of landing in a three-point fashion, and never felt like they wanted to drop a wing. A three-pointer was guaranteed as long as you flew a decent curved approach and flattened out just before touching down.

'We encountered serious problems with the prop torque of the Mk XIV, and pilots soon found that because of the type's heavy wing loading (due to the cannon and camera gear) you couldn't open the throttle to more than zero boost on take-off because if you went over that on an initial run the aircraft ground-looped. Once airborne the fighter climbed away like a rocket. However, because of the excessive wing loading we were restricted to a dive speed of 369 knots, as it was calculated that the wings might part company with the fuselage if too much speed was built up. Talking to pilots at Duxford today who fly the Mk XIV stripped of all this operational equipment, they can take-off on grass or concrete with +4 or +5 boost pressure without any adverse affects on the fighter's handling!

'The FR XIV was essentially a flying engine, and this was never more obvious than when one performed aerobatics. I attempted to master the aircraft in this flying regime once we had been sent to Germany as part of the force of occupation – we were

BELOW Although at first glance this trio of No 17 Sqn F XIVEs (photographed on a sortie from Seletar, Singapore, in September 1945) all appear to be indentically marked, a closer inspection reveals differences between each of them. 'TB-E' (RN152) still retains Fighter Command's sky blue 'fighter band' around its fuselage (actually deleted globally by the RAF in January 1945, but still worn on many aircraft well past VE-Day), as applied at the factory in England – hence the application of the aircraft's serial in black.

'YB-C' (RN205) has had the band painted over and the distinctive SEAC horizontal white bar added to its vertical surface, the latter reducing the fin flash by over 50 per cent. The removal of the 'fighter band' has also meant that its serial had to be reapplied in white to match its squadron codes. The last of the trio – 'YB-H' – has an indistinguishable serial inexplicably applied in black, despite having had the fuselage band removed and the fin bar applied. Furthermore, it is the only one of the three to boast a No 17 Sqn badge on its engine cowling (*Don Healey*)

ABOVE An anonymous Spitfire F XIVE cruises high over the clouds of southern England in the spring of 1944, its Griffon engine singing out a reassuringly throaty 'growl' as the pilot edges his mount ever closer the photographer. Like the later marks of Merlin Spitfire, all Griffon-powered machines had a symmetrical radiator layout on the wing undersurfaces

assigned to No 127 Wg at Lübeck, commanded by Grp Capt "Johnnie" Johnson, on VJ-Day. The first loop I ever attempted in the aircraft was the most shuddering affair I can ever remember, as you had to "motor" the machine around on the Griffon engine throughout the manoeuvre – it really was a most unpleasant experience. Conversely, its rate of roll was astounding! The Mk XIV truly is a "man's aeroplane", as Stephen Grey of The Fighter Collection describes it, and it was plainly obvious to me back in 1945 why so many inexperienced pilots found the Griffon Spitfires so daunting to fly, having come from an OTU equipped with Merlin-powered Mk Vs and IXs.

'In the low-level recce role that we operated the FR XIVs in, the aircraft excelled, with the bubble canopy offering the pilot virtually unlimited visibility both forward and aft – this feature was particularly useful for our secondary task of artillery spotting. Our CO at the time, Sqn Ldr Pat Cleary, drummed into us that we should always fire our cameras first, not our guns, if we encountered the enemy, as it was information that our Army colleagues wanted.

'We flew a figure-eight pattern when we were assigned artillery-spotting duties. We would fly out with the fall of shot from the long-range guns, relaying direction information to them as every salvo landed. Once accuracy had been achieved, we would relay a message to this effect, and head off to the next target.

'I flew a total of 90 hours in the FR XIV, flying hourly sorties from Lübeck, which was sighted right on the Russian border in eastern Germany. We weren't flying any specific missions whilst based here, just routine patrols along the border, and this allowed me to get very familiar with the aircraft. It was very much like a racehorse, powering along with its great Griffon engine up front. I always looked forward to flying the machine, despite the fact that we were not flying operational sorties in the truest sense.'

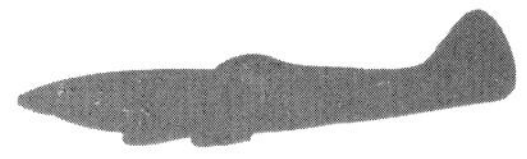

YB A

PREVIOUS PAGES AND RIGHT The most impressive of all surviving Supermarine fighters 'on the wing' today is The Fighter Collection's (TFC) F XIVE SM832 was an important addition to the global ranks of the airworthy Spitfire community in 1995 – particularly in light of the tragic loss of RM689 on 26 June 1992, which had been the only airworthy 'high back' Mk XIV in the world for many years. Seen in this sequence of photographs with Stephen Grey at the controls, SM832 has been restored at TFC and finished by Historic Flying Ltd as Sqn Ldr 'Ginger' Lacey's 'YB-A' (RN135) of No 17 Sqn in mid-1945.

Built at Chattis Hill, near Winchester, in early 1945, SM832 was delivered to No 29 MU at High Ercall on 13 March. Like many other F XIVEs built around this time, it was soon allocated to SEAC and crated up and shipped to India – it was despatched to Bombay aboard the *Highland Prince* in April 1945. With the war in the Far East having swung firmly in favour of the Allies by the time SM832 turned up in-theatre, the fighter's chance of a frontline career was limited. Placed in storage for two years, it was finally passed on to the Indian Air Force (IAF) in July 1947. Like virtually all other Spitfires that followed this route, its service career with the IAF remains unresearched

YB A

LEFT SM832 was one of five Spitfires (four Mk XIVs and a Mk XVIII) brought out of India by the late Doug Arnold for his Warbirds of Great Britain collection in the late 1970s, having been discovered serving as a gate guard at Dehra Dun. Reported by the recovery team to be in remarkably good condition despite its lengthy spell outdoors, the fighter was shipped back to the UK in 1979 and stored at Blackbushe for a number of years, before being acquired by TFC. After a thorough overhaul at Duxford and final completion at Audley End, its first test flight was performed from the Essex airstrip on the evening of 22 May 1995, with Air Marshal Sir John Allison performing the honours.

Seen here on a practice sortie prior to the world famous *Flying Legends* Airshow of 15/16 July, SM832 leads TFC's second Mk XIV (MV393), flown by Jack Brown. Making its public debut at Duxford that weekend, SM832 easily 'stole the show' thanks to Stephen Grey's stunning display graphically illustrating just why the Mk XIV has been described as the 'flying engine'

ABOVE AND RIGHT Like SM832, TFC's other superbly restored Griffon Spitfire – FR XIVE MV293 – was also an ex-Indian Air Force machine retrieved in outstanding and complete condition from Bangalore by Doug Arnold and his team in 1979. It had been built at Keevil in January 1945, but sat in storage until being crated up and shipped to India aboard the *Dee Bank* in September of that year. It too was transferred to the IAF in late December 1947, and like its hangar-mate, no records have been found of its frontline career with the Indians. Acquired by TFC in 1985, MV293 was restored in-house at Duxford and test flown for the first time from the Cambridgeshire airfield on 14 August 1992 by Stephen Grey. Resprayed as a No 2 Sqn F XIVC based at Wahn, in Germany, in late 1945, the fighter is being flown at right by Jack Brown and above by Peter Kynsey

BELOW Propeller blades to the fore, a gaggle of securely-tethered Spitfire F XIVEs of No 132 Sqn provide a backdrop to an impromptu session of gymnastics aboard HMS *Smiter* en route to Hong Kong on 1 November 1945

INTERCOOLANT

NH799
V
AP

THIS SPREAD The third in the trio of ex-Warbirds of Great Britain Griffon Spitfires acquired by TFC in the mid-1980s was NH799, a rare elliptically-winged FR XIV built at Aldermaston in early 1945. Although like the other aircraft featured in this chapter it was sent to SEAC, NH799 actually saw frontline service with the RAF, reportedly being issued to either Nos 9 or 49 Sqns, depending on which source you believe! Both of these units were part of Bomber Command at the time, and neither saw service with SEAC when NH799 was in-theatre, so reports pertaining to its RAF career may not be totally accurate. According to Air Ministry records it suffered a Cat E flying accident on 27 February 1947 whilst serving with No 9 Sqn, although the same source fails to indicate if it was repaired prior to its transfer to the IAF in December of that year.

In this stunning sequence of shots taken in the environs of Wanaka, in New Zealand, in 1994, NH799 is being flown by the OFMC's Mark Hanna

RIGHT Although NH799 was one the last ex-Indian Spitfire to be recovered by Doug Arnold, it was easily on e of the best preserved. The Spitfire arrived at the latter's Blackbushe base in 1981, and was shifted to Bitteswell in mid-1985, where it was acquired by TFC in a deal that saw all four of Arnold's Mk XIVs change ownership. It was structurally and mechanically restored by its new owners and finished at Historic Flying Ltd. Again, it was Air Marshal Sir John Allison who performed NH799's post-restoration test flight from Audley End on 21 January 1994. It was then sold to Sir Tim Wallis and shipped to Wanaka later that same year.

Cruising over wispy clouds, Mark Hanna edges NH799 in towards the camera-ship, and thus shows off the fighter's elliptical wing planform. Compare its 'E' wing armament configuration, which sees its .5-in Browning machine guns fitted inboard of its 20 mm cannon, with the opposite arrangement adopted on TFC's earlier F XIVC MV293.

NH799 was severely damaged in a flying accident at Wanaka on New Year's Day 1996

LEFT AND RIGHT Mark Hanna continues to enjoy himself in the crystalline skies over the Southern Alps of New Zealand's rugged South Island in 1994

ABOVE Seen in April 1994 just prior to the *Warbirds over Wanaka* event, NH799 (with Mark Hanna at the controls) leads Spitfire LF XVIE TB863 (flown by father Ray) over South Island farmland. Both aircraft are part of the Alpine Fighter Collection, the latter machine having arrived in New Zealand in 1989. NH799 wears the codes of a No 130 Sqn 'high-back' F XIV based at Lympne as part of the 'anti-*Diver*' force protecting London from V1 attacks in August 1944 – the unit downed 11.5 'Doodlebugs' whilst assigned this hazardous duty. Note the CO's pennant beneath the cockpit, the squadron's boss during this period being Sqn Ldr P V K Tripe, DFC, RCAF

CHAPTER SEVEN

PACKARD MERLIN SPITFIRE

Spitfire LF Mk XVIEs RW382 and TB863

Flight Lieutenant Raymond Baxter
No 602 Squadron
July 1944 to May 1945

'I was very familiar with the Spitfire by the time I arrived in Normandy to join No 602 'City of Glasgow' Sqn, and I later became its A Flight commander. I had already completed one-and-a-half tours on the type, flying Mk IIs, Vs and Mk IXs with Nos 65 (in the UK in 1941/42, Ed.) and 93 Sqns, the latter unit serving as a forward squadron "in the field" throughout the North African campaign, before moving to Malta and then participating in the invasion of Sicily and Salerno, prior to heading north to Naples.

'Of all the marks I flew in four solid years of Spitfire flying, my undisputed favourite was the clipped-wing XVI. This was due primarily to the fact that "I came good" on this mark, profiting from previous frontline experience to enjoy total confidence in the aircraft in a wide variety of combat environments. We did a lot of dive-bombing in the final year of the war, and I wasn't too bad at that – I often flew as formation leader. Performing this style of attack also gave me immense satisfaction, as I felt that I was contributing something towards combating the final German threat, albeit in a rather limited fashion in a single-seat fighter hurriedly converted to drop bombs with considerable precision.

'This positive feeling of hitting the enemy where it hurt may have come from having spent many long hours performing bomber escort missions whilst being shot at by flak batteries sometimes thousands of feet below. It was a hell of a motivator to know that every time you took off from July 1944 until VE-Day you were going to give someone a "whack in the eye".

'Although there is some diversity of opinion on the adequacy of the Spitfire XVI to undertake dive-bombing missions, we evolved our own technique on the squadron which served us very well indeed. The leading instigator of this was our intrepid CO, Sqn Ldr Max Sutherland, who served two tours in command of the unit.'

He had commanded No 602 Sqn from October 1943 through to July 1944, until replaced by seasoned 18-kill ace, South African 'Chris' Le Roux , who took charge of the unit in July. He soon made his mark by downing three Bf 109Gs and two Fw 190s within a week of his arrival.

Sadly, Le Roux's reign was to be a short-lived one for he was lost in bad weather over the Channel whilst attempting to fly from Normandy to England on 29 August 1944. Veteran Flight Commander 'Bob' Stewart assumed command, and a month later, following their courageous efforts in support of the Arnhem fiasco, No 602 Sqn returned to Coltishall for re-equipment with some of the first Spitfires LF XVIEs to reach the RAF. Max Sutherland, starting his fifth frontline

BELOW Flt Lt Raymond Baxter prepares for his next sorite over Holland in 'his' Spitfire LF XVIE, which he christened *Sylvia M* (*Raymond Baxter*)

ABOVE Huddled around a well-used large-scale map of Holland, No 602 Sqn pilots scour the area for recognisible features that match the V2 target photos recently handed to them by the Ops officer. Second from left is Flt Lt Baxter, who appears to have spotted something of interest in the centre of the map (*Raymond Baxter*)

tour, led them back to Norfolk. Raymond Baxter continues the story;

'Unlike our ageing Mk IXEs, the new Mk XVIs were fitted with gyro gunsights, which we were totally unfamiliar with. Despite our ignorance, we were simply issued with the aircraft and had to learn very quickly! Fortunately, our experiences over the "killing fields" of the Falaise Gap had taught us how to use the Spitfire effectively in the ground attack role, and we soon devised an absurdly simple technique that allowed us to make full use of the gyro sight.

'Once committed to the attack, you throttled back to 200 mph and let the target pass under the wing just inboard of the roundel. As it emerged from under the wing you would count to three, roll on your back and pull the Spitfire into a 70° dive, keeping the target in full view. Of course an attack at this angle made you feel as if you were diving at the ground vertically, which was made worse if you were not quite steep enough and you had to push the nose down even more! Once trimmed, and with the throttle pulled back, the Mk XVI held very steady when hurtling groundward, which allowed you to make full use of the excellent Mk II gunsight, and thus achieve impressive levels of accuracy.

'The graticule was brought to bear on the target, and all instrument readings and flak burst were ignored for the duration of the dive. One had to avoid side-slipping, skidding to dodge the AA or turning whilst in this phase of the attack as they all adversely affected your aim. The squadron usually attacked in a loose line astern formation, with 20 to 30 yards separation. Each pilot was responsible for lining up the target, releasing his own bomb and recovering after the attack.

'We never really monitored our dive speeds during these attacks – I think 360 mph was a typical maximum velocity achieved, remembering that we had our engines throttle back throughout the dive – and I can't ever remember being told what the "never exceed" speed was! On several occasions Spitfires from other 2nd Tactical Air Force (TAF) squadrons broke up or shed wings in diving attacks, but that was usually when the bombs failed to unstick, and the 'g' force exerted on the flying surfaces during the pull out exceeded the design's maximum wing loading. Unfortunately, you only discovered that your bombs had "stuck" once you pulled the stick back to level out.

'On the topic of dive recovery, to avoid overstressing our aircraft we adopted the tactic of flattening out the bottom of the dive into a 5g pull by continuing to go down after we had salvoed our bombs at 2500 ft – the lowest altitude at which bombs could be released in a dive was 1500 ft, but that meant a high-g pull-up straight after your bombs had gone. We would level out at about 100 ft and make our escape at tree-top height. The great temptation of course was to climb out from the attack to see how accurate you had been in delivering your ordnance, but the German gunners knew their stuff so this manoeuvre was discouraged. Our job was to go in tight, hit hard and get the Hell out of harm's way as quickly as possible.

'The usual armament for these sorties was a single 250-lb bomb under each wing, and a 500-lb device on the centreline, which were usually all dropped at once. These weapons often had delayed action fuses fitted to them, which could be set not to explode for up to six hours. The firing mechanism on these bombs was triggered when the copper plate protecting it had been eaten through by acid contained in a phial within the weapon's casing. This chemical reaction was set in motion by squadron armourers immediately prior to take-off, and I was constantly aware of this primitive device fizzing aware beneath me.

'We also performed a considerable amount of "skip bombing" during this period, which I enjoyed immensely. The attack profile for these sorties was very simple – fly as low as you dared at the target in question (often a bridge or embankment) and just let the weapons go. The forward moment of the aircraft carried the bomb along, and the 11-second delay fuse normally fitted allowed you sufficient time to get away before the weapon detonated. On one occasion, however, I had a bomb explode as soon as it hit the ground, which didn't half frighten me, but fortunately my Spitfire survived the blast better than I did!

'The Spitfire had a reputation for not withstanding damage to its all-important coolant system, so I was always extremely conscious of the engine temperature and oil pressure.'

V2 busting

One of the primary reasons for No 602 Sqn's return to the UK in late September from Belgium, and the 2nd TAF, was that they had been earmarked to take on Hitler's final terror weapon, the V2, in a campaign code-named *No Ball*. The first of these had hit London earlier that month, and it was soon realised that the only way to combat this deadly weapon was to hit its mobile launch sites. Raymond Baxter explains further;

'Together with the similarly-equipped Nos 229, 453 and 603 Sqns, we were given the task of maintaining vigorous patrol activity over the areas from which the rockets were coming, mainly round The Hague – we dubbed our quarry "Big Ben" sites. If V2 activity was spotted we were given the clearance to sort it out immediately, but the Germans were masters at camouflaging these extremely mobile sites. In an attempt to keep the pressure on the enemy, we were given a wide-ranging brief, and as we knew that the Germans were short on fuel, any vehicle caught on the roads in Holland was invariably assisting the war effort. We therefore "shot at anything that moved", but went to great pains not to endanger Dutch lives.

'We also carried out pre-planned strikes on rocket storage areas and launch site, based on information fed to us by the Dutch resistance. We often had to rely on their accurate assessments of these targets as from the air little more than wheel tracks at most could be seen. Our usual force on a typical anti-V2 mission consisted of four to six Spitfires loaded with a single 500 and two 250 lb bombs, or alternatively just the latter and a centreline fuel tank. Once we had departed Coltishall, or its satellites at Matlaske, Ludham or Swannington (where we operated for much of the campaign), we headed over the North Sea, climbing to 8000 ft.

'As a formation leader, one had one's hands full navigating a bloody long way over an expanse of water that had already claimed our previous CO just a matter of weeks before. Our navigational aids consisted exclusively of a map and a compass, and visual aids in the North Sea are rather few and far between! We quickly got to know the shape of the sand banks off the Norfolk coast, however, which gave us the means to check our drift since setting course after take-off and forming up.

'As we crossed the enemy coastline, we were traditionally greeted by flak thrown up by heavy 88 mm AA batteries, although these were easily evaded in a Spitfire as long as one continually altered direction and altitude in a series of long gently climbing or diving turns. The V2 sites themselves were guarded by light flak, and we would vary our attack profiles to suit the weather and target layout. Occasionally we would attack straight away, whilst on other sorties we would dodge in and out of cloud until in the most favourable position to attack. Our last strike method was to overfly the target as if we hadn't seen it, then reverse course a little way away and come in out of the sun.

'On one mission I remember vividly, we caught the V2 crew well into their launch countdown. We had already dropped our bombs, and my "Number Four", who now prefers to remain nameless, had turned back into the target to perform a strafing attack when the V2 came climbing out of the clump of trees immediately in front of us, belching flame. He re-sighted his guns and fired a long burst at the rocket, but fortunately his attempts at becoming the first person to shoot down a ballistic missile in flight met with failure, as the resulting explosion might well have taken all six Spitfires down with it!

'Probably the most "press on" op I ever participated in was the raid on the Baatasher-Mex office building, situated in the middle of The Hague, on 18 March 1945 – its originator, our CO Max Sutherland (who really was an inspirational leader), got a bar to his DFC for completing this trip.

'It all started when word came through from Dutch intelligence that the technical HQ for the V2 force in Holland was located here. Max persuaded Group that No 602 Sqn could deliver a precision strike on the site, without inflicting damage on the civilian populous of the city. He handpicked a team of six pilots, and we teamed up with the Aussies of No 453 Sqn, led by Sqn Ldr 'Ernie' Esau, who would provide a diversionary strike for us by bombing a known "Big Ben" site in the middle of the city's racecourse using their identical LF XVIEs (it was estimated that there were 200+ flak batteries lining the route to the target, Ed.).

'In order to minimise civilian casualties we had to launch our skip bomb attack from window height in a tight line abreast formation – the number of Spitfires chosen for the job had been dictated by the width of the building. With the diversionary strike in full swing, the six of us dived in with a lot of power on wing tip to wing tip. It looked damn impressive!

'Flak was flying up at us but we all kept together in a rock-steady formation with our guns firing, until the CO gave the word to release the delayed-fuse bombs. Once they were gone I looked up beyond the target for the first time since we had started the attack run and immediately spotted a tall church spire in my path! I was sandwiched in by the CO to my left and Steve Stephenson to my right, so all I could do was yank the stick back. I swear to this day that the cockerel atop the spire passed under my wing by a matter of inches.

'As we shot north of the city at zero feet, Max pulled up to look back and drew a lot of flak – whether he did this to protect the rest of us, I shall never know. We all managed to land safely at an RAF-manned airstrip near Ghent, in Belgium, where the undamaged Spitfires were re-armed and refuelled. The boss's aircraft had lost a lot of its rudder and had had its starboard elevator turned into a colander. Earlier that same day I had skip-bombed a road bridge north of Gouda, and following our brief interlude on the ground we executed a low-level interdiction sortie against traffic on the railway line between Delft and Rotterdam on the way home – I earned my pay that day.

'The clipped wing on the LF XVIE made the aircraft a delight to reef about at low-level. It was easily the most offensively-optimised Spitfire I ever flew, and the old Packard-Merlin was a great engine for the job, with one exception. There was a rev range in which it didn't run smoothly, and of course this was the range we had habitually used for long-range formation work in order to conserve fuel. The only solution was to avoid those revs, and the problem, I was later told by the great Sir Stanley Hooker of Rolls-Royce, was caused by Packard using a slightly modified carburettor.

'After our escapades over The Hague, we did several long-range daylight escorts to both RAF and USAAF heavy bombers attacking targets that included Peenemunde and Heligoland, plus covered the liberation of the Channel Islands, amongst other adventures. Eleven days after VE-Day, my squadron was disbanded. Indeed, the Ministry of Supply sent *girls* to take our Spitfires away. They were, of course, the gallant and glamourous ladies of the Air Transport Auxiliary (ATA), of whom I now number several as personal friends of both my wife and myself, but at the time we were so angry at this we couldn't even make a pass at them. I was then promptly packed onto a Dakota and posted overseas *again*, where I converted onto Mustang IVs, in order to fly them from Cairo to India using Mosquitos as pathfinders for the gathering *Tiger Force*.

'Our American allies had always claimed that the P-51 was a "hot ship" when compared to the Spitfire, primarily because it came in "over the hedge" at 120 rather than 90, but that caused us novice Mustang pilots no dramas at all. There is no doubting that the P-51 was a great aircraft to fly, boasting a superb laminar-flow wing, huge range and well-proportioned cockpit. We ex-Spitfire pilots appreciated the latter enormously because after three-and-a-half hours in a Spitfire cockpit on a long-range bomber escort sortie, one's lower half was well and truly "seized up".

'That said, I wouldn't have traded my Mk IX or my LF XVIE for any other Allied fighter. Every Spitfire I flew was different, with its own unique little foibles. For example, if your own machine went unserviceable and you were forced to take somebody else's, you could feel the difference the moment you were airborne. You didn't get that feeling of individuality with the Mustang. Simply put, I would not have wanted to operate any other type of aircraft in wartime.'

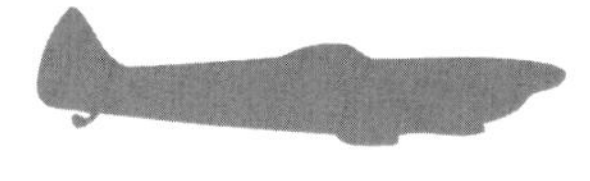

ABOVE Built at Castle Bromwich in mid-1945, this natural-metal LF XVIE was issued to the RAF too late to see service with a frontline unit. After a short spell in storage, it was sent to the Central Gunnery School at Leconfield, where it performed tirelessly for almost three years before suffering engine failure over the West Skipsea Ranges on 6 January 1949, and being written-off in the subsequent forced landing

THIS SPREAD Much of Historic Flying Ltd's handiwork has been on display for all to see in this volume, and of the dozen or so Spitfires the company has restored over the past seven years, this particular LF XVIE (RW382) was the first to return to the skies on 3 July 1991. Indeed, this very aircraft was at the centre of the 'great gate guard swap' of 1988 between the MoD and Cambridge businessman Tim Routsis. As one of five Spitfires obtained by the latter, it was chosen as the first to be restored for it had been 'pre-sold' to collector David Tallichet of Chino, California. In return the latter supplied the derelict P-40 Kittyhawk and rare Bristol Beaufort that the RAF Museum at Hendon so desperately wanted – and had convinced the MoD to swap five Spitfire gate guards for.

At left, Tim Routsis is seen flying RW832 in 1992, whilst in the close-up on the right Air Marshal Sir John Allison (RW382's test pilot) is at the controls

LEFT AND INSET Like a great number of 'bubble-top' Mk XVIs, RW382 rolled off the Castle Bromwich line just too late to see combat with the RAF. Stored between July 1945 and April 1947, it was finally retrieved from its dormant state at Brize Norton and issued to No 604 'County of Middlesex' Sqn at Hendon. Here it remained until April 1950, when the unit transitioned to Vampire F.3s and disposed of its Spitfires.

Storage at Lyneham came to an end in June 1951 when it was sent to No 3 Civilian Anti-Aircraft Co-operation Unit, followed four months later by a transfer to the Control and Reporting School at Middle Wallop. Finally retired on 14 July 1953 to Kinloss, it was issued a year later to No 609 'West Riding Sqn as an instructional airframe, prior to commencing its 30-year association with gate guard duties. Breaking away from the camera at left is Charlie Brown, whilst climbing skyward below is Air Marshal Sir John Allison

RIGHT RW382 spent 12 years on the gate at RAF Leconfield, where it had to suffer the ignominy of wearing an incorrect serial and codes – 'RW729/DW-X'. In 1967 it was loaned to Spitfire Productions and moved to Henlow where it was made taxiable for filming during *The Battle of Britain* shoot. Returned to Leconfield in December 1969, it was moved to RAF Kemble soon afterwards for refurbishment, which included a respray in 1940-period Fighter Command colours!

RW382 was then trucked down to RAF Uxbridge in April 1973 and pylon-mounted adjacent to the main gate. There it stayed until Tim Routsis convinced the MoD to replace its gate guard Spitfires with plastic replicas, and allow him to restore the former to airworthiness. Of the five machine obtained by Historic Flying, RW382 was reported to be in the best physical state thanks to sound corrosion-inhibition performed in the early 1970s. It was removed from its pole in August 1988 and moved to Audley End, where restoration got underway that autumn.

Part of the deal agreed with David Tallichet saw RW382 (finished in the scheme it wore with No 604 Sqn) retained at Historic Flying for several years, during which time both Tim Routsis and fellow company founder, Clive Denney, used the fighter to perform their first solo flights in a Spitfire. It was finally crated up and sent to California in late 1994, and has since been sold on to a Canadian collector.

Charlie Brown is seen here flying RW382 over broken cloud near Cambridge in mid-1992

NG C
RW382

TB

LEFT Set against the dramatically lit landscape of the Southern Alps, Sir Tim Wallis weaves his immaculate Spitfire LF XVIE from side to side in order to keep tabs on the snow-covered peaks ahead of him

LEFT AND INSET

With its pointed fin tip, high-back fuselage and 'E' wing, it is difficult to distinguish between TB863 and a late-build Mk IX. However, one look under the engine cowls will confirm that beneath its skin beats a 'heart' made of Detroit steel in the form of Rolls-Royce Packard Merlin 266 – identical to the powerplant fitted into the fighter at Castle Bromwich in early 1945.

TB863's career has been a long and varied one, ranging from anti-V2 sorties over Holland with No 485 Sqn, RAAF (in whose colours it is presently finished), to film work as a stage prop in MGM's *Reach for the Sky*, shot a decade later.

Following its part in creating celluloid history, TB863 languished at Pinewood Studios until briefly called upon to provide further spares for *The Battle of Britain* Spitfire fleet in 1967 – its major contribution was to provide Mk IA AR213 with its centre spar

THIS SPREAD Sold off as little more than a gutted and engineless hulk soon after its film work was completed, TB863 was moved to a number of sites over the next 14 years before ending up at PPS at Booker, where a steady restoration commenced. It was purchased partly restored by Stephen Grey in the early 1980s, and although its wings remained at PPS under rebuild, the bulk of the aircraft was trucked to Duxford. In February 1986 a thorough rework was started that saw all its internal fittings stripped, many panels and rivets replaced and crack testing and corrosion treatment carried out, prior to replacement skins being fitted.

Final fitting out commenced in July 1987, and an overhauled Packard Merlin 266 engine and zero-houred prop completed the job in January 1988. By this stage it had been bought by the Alpine Fighter Collection, who had it shipped to New Zealand later that year following its initial test flights from Duxford. TB863 has remained a firm favourite with Wanaka crowds ever since, and is seen here with Sir Tim Wallis in the cockpit

CHAPTER EIGHT

JUNGLE SPITFIRE

Spitfire FR Mk XVIIIE TP280

Flying Officer John Nicholls
No 28 Squadron
May 1948 to June 1949

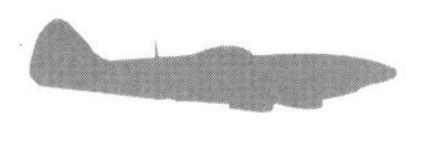

'In June 1948, when the State of Emergency was declared in Malaya, I was a 21-year-old Flying Officer serving with No 28 Fighter Reconnaissance Squadron which operated Spitfire XVIIIs from Sembawang, on Singapore Island. With those of the similarly-equipped No 60 Sqn, there was a total of 16 Spitfires in Malaya – these, and a few Beaufighters and Sunderlands, made up the Royal Air Force's entire offensive strength in the area.

'Almost from the start we, and the other squadrons, began sending out strikes against the jungle hide-outs used by the terrorists. In the beginning it was a rather hit and miss affair, with one far more likely to miss than hit. The maps we carried were almost devoid of detail, except along the coast – they would show dominant features such as rivers, but after a short distance inland these would peter out into a dotted line, with the helpful caption "It is assumed that the river follows this line"! The reconnaissance Spitfires of No 81 Sqn would take target photographs for us, but since their maps were the same as our own, they had similar problems of navigation. In the jungle one tree-covered hill can look depressingly like a thousand others.

'I vividly remember the first time I dropped a bomb in anger. On 2 July 1948 I went off with my squadron commander, Sqn Ldr Bob Yule (a Kiwi, Yule was a veteran wartime pilot who had scored three kills and shared five more during his career in Fighter Command, which commenced in October 1939 – sadly he was killed on 11 September 1953 in a collision between two Meteor F.8s during a Battle of Britain flypast rehearsal over London, Ed.), to a target just across the causeway from Singapore, in South Johore. We took off at first light so that we could get in our dive attacks before the usual mid-morning layer of cumulous cloud developed. When we reached the target area we cruised round for more than half-an-hour looking for something resembling our briefed objective, before we eventually attacked. Diving from 12,000 ft, we dropped our 500 pounders, two from each aircraft, then we carried out a series of strafing runs with cannon and machine guns. There was nobody firing back – it really was like being on the range, except that the target was far less distinct.

'During the months that followed we flew several

BELOW FR XVIIIE TP448 was photographed on a patrol over Cyprus (performed from its Nicosia base) in 1949, and it wears the 'GZ' codes of No 32 Sqn. The additional '?' was a favourite marking adopted by units in the Middle East in 1941, and was perpetuated within 'old and bold' Fighter Command squadrons well into the postwar age

similar strikes. Most of the targets were in deep jungle, and sometimes half a dozen of us would circle for up to an hour looking for the hut, or whatever it was we were supposed to hit. Then the first pilot who reckoned he had found it would bomb, and the rest of us would follow and aim at his bursts. After that we would strafe the area until we had used up our ammunition. At that time our intelligence on the whereabouts of the enemy was poor. Moreover, only rarely could our troops go in to find out what the air strikes had achieved. Sometimes, a week or so after the attack we might hear that the target "basha" hut had been hit by cannon shells, but by the time the ground forces reached it there was rarely any sign of the actual terrorists.

'It was all rather loose and inconclusive, and the reasons were not difficult to understand. Guerrilla fighters make the maximum use of all available cover. They travel light, move fast and seldom concentrate. Operating in dense jungle, they are extremely difficult to find. Broadly speaking, air attacks against them can be mounted in two distinct ways – precision attacks or area attacks. Precision attacks, by definition, require the target to be visible, or to be marked in some way. Area attacks demand a great weight of attack to saturate the area. And both depend for their success upon up-to-date intelligence on the target.

'The ineffectiveness of the Spitfire in these operations illustrates the sort of problem we had using an interceptor designed 13 years earlier to bomb such difficult targets. Later, Lincoln heavy bombers equipped with radar took over the task of attacking the jungle hideouts, but even with their much greater bomb loads I am not convinced that they achieved much. Indeed, as Vietnam has shown, one needs a bomber the size of the B-52, laying down patterns of up to 84 500 pounders, before one can make any real impression on the jungle – and even then, as I have said, one needs first-class intelligence if one is to really hit the enemy.

'I left No 28 Sqn in mid-1949, before the Malayan operations were placed on a proper footing. I had had a lot of fun, but had not, I think, done all that much to help defeat the terrorists.

'Operating against the guerrillas in Malaya, we were really asking too much from the Spitfire. But I have no doubts regarding its value as an air fighter. It had that rare quality which comes from a perfect matching of control responsiveness and "feel", which made the aircraft part of you once you were airborne. You strapped on, rather than got into, a Spitfire. Your hand on the stick produced instant control reaction, and it would obey as accurately and almost as quickly as one's right arm obeys the command from the brain. I have known a few other aircraft with this highly personal characteristic – the Vampire and the Hunter, followed by the F-104A Starfighter which, despite its outstanding performance in terms of speed, retained that same unique quality as a perfect fighter pilot's aeroplane. But for me the Spitfire was the first, and so the one best loved.'

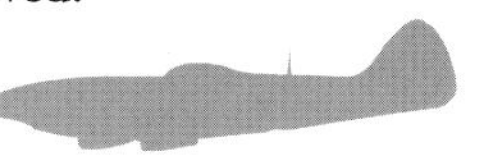

TOP AND ABOVE Two standard factory shots reveal all the salient details of 'Super Spitfire' FR XVIIIE TP265, which was sent to SEAC soon after VJ-Day, and was later sold to the Indian Air Force

LEFT The sheer size of the Griffon 67 engine fitted into the FR XVIIIE can be clearly gauged when compared with these two No 28 Sqn groundcrew, taking a break from servicing the 'beast' in the hot Singaporean sun at Sembawang in February 1948

NG
C
RW382
Z

LEFT Two examples of Historic Flying's Spitfire 'craft' formate over Cambridgeshire in 1992 – flying FR XVIIIE TP280 is its owner Rudy Frasca, of Frasca Sumulation, whilst his wingman in LF XVIE RW382 is Charlie Brown.

Built by Supermarine at Soutnampton in 1945, TP280 was despatched to India soon after its acceptance by the RAF, and like many other late-build Griffon Spitfires, Its service in the Far East has not yet been researched. TP280 was transferred to Indian control in 1948, and there it remained until offered for sale by its owners, along witrh a number of other Spitfires

ABOVE TP280 was soon bought by Ormond and Wensley Haydon-Baillie, along with seven other airframes, and in turn sold (along with FR XVIIIE TP276) to Rudy Frasca and shipped to his Champaign, Illinois, base

LEFT Once returned to airworthiness in 1992, the Spitfire was resprayed in a distinctive No 60 Sqn 'Malayan Crisis' scheme, after which its Fighter Command band was signed by a number of ex-No 60 Sqn pilots, plus Jeffrey Quill

RIGHT A slow restoration was then commenced on TP280, and steady progress was made until its owner decided to ship the aircraft to Audley End in late 1990 for Historic Flying to complete the job – work in the UK was overseen by Geoff Hughes. By 5 July 1992 the Spitfire was ready for its first flight, which was duly conducted by seasoned Spitfire test pilot, Air Marshal Sir John Allison. Appearing publicly just the once at a Duxford airshow during the summer of that year, TP280 returned to Frasca Field, in Illinois, in early September 1992, and has been a star performer at many an event across the Mid-West ever since – Frasca Sumulation are currently restoring TP276 to airworthiness as this book went to press.

As previously mentioned, TP280 has been sprayed up in No 60 Sqn colours as worn by the unit's FR XVIIIEs between 1949 and 1952. 'Z' was the OC's aircraft, flown by wartime ace, Sqn Ldr Wilfred Duncan-Smith, DSO, DFC, who led the squadron on anti-guerilla sweeps of the Malayan jungle during the country's 'crisis' – his signature can today be found on the 'fighter band' on TP280's fuselage. The Spitfire fired its guns for the last time in anger whilst in Malaya with No 60 Sqn

Z
TP280

WARTIME GALLERY

ABOVE Sqn Ldr John J Lynch, DFC and Bar, sits in a Spitfire VC of No 249 Sqn at Ta Kali, on Malta, in mid-1942

LEFT Spitfire I P9386 of No 19 Sqn at Fowlmere in September 1940

LEFT Spitfire VB EN821 of No 243 Sqn, based at Turnhouse, in September 1942

LEFT No 611 'West Lancashire' Sqn pilots at Biggin Hill with a Spitfire F IXC in May 1943

BELOW Spitfire VB W3238 *The London Butcher* and No 609 'West Rding' Sqn pilots at Biggin Hill in June 1941

RIGHT Spitfire LF VIII of No 601 'County of London' Sqn in Italy in early 1944

RIGHT An anonymous Spitfire LF IXC somewhere in England in early 1944

ABOVE No 611 'County of West Lancashire' Sqn Spitfire F IXCs over the East End of London in late 1942

BELOW Sgt J P Wilson of No 222 Sqn sits in Spitfire Mk VB W3253 *Central Provinces and Berar VI* at Southend in July 1941

LEFT No 43 Sqn Spitfire LF VIII in southern France in August 1944

A J (Andy) Sephton
Test Pilot for Rolls-Royce, Bristol, 1989-96
Display Pilot for the Shuttleworth Trust, 1992-96

'I first flew the Spitfire (a Mk XIV owned by Rolls-Royce) on 2 August 1989 – 22 years to the day after my first solo flight, which took place in a Cessna 150 at Carlisle airport. It had been a long wait to realise my childhood dream! Since then I've been fortunate enough to fly five different marks covering clipped and round wing tips, low and high back, small and large fin and Merlin and Griffon variants.

'Each has its own characteristics. For example, the power of the Griffon makes the later marks most impressive in the speed and acceleration stakes, but increases cockpit noise and torque – the latter makes achieving balanced flight a severe test of pilot co-ordination. The low back increases cockpit field of view (visibility is the distance one can see from the cockpit, field of view is the area one can scan), but reduces directional stability markedly. The larger finned variants do help in providing more lateral control power, but the large fin always arrived later than the previous modification that required its design in the first place!

'Clipped wings increase the roll rate, reduce drag and greatly enhance the handling qualities of the aircraft near the stall. Against this is the increased stall speed, and associated longer landing distance, increased turn rate and, most importantly, the destruction of that unique shape that characterises this aircraft – the elliptical wing. In general, the earlier the mark, the better the handling qualities, whilst the later the mark, the more the engine power available.

'Which is my favourite? They all are!

'The brute power and noise of the Griffon in the Mk XIV is a total contrast to the relatively quiet, lightweight, Mk V, and each gives its own satisfaction when displayed appropriately.

'The Shuttleworth Collection's LF Mk VC has been a regular performer throughout the summer season at Old Warden since 1975. Here, it is part of a unique display that showcases aircraft from the beginnings of powered aviation like the Blackburn of 1912, for example, through World War 1 types such as the Sopwith Pup and Triplane, to the interwar years with the Hawker Hind and Gloster Gladiator, before finishing off with the Spitfire. Hopping from one cockpit to another can be a most gratifying experience, especially as one can experience the classic machines of yesteryear in one afternoon.

'Comparing them, however, can be a nightmare. It is easy to fix on and criticise the poor directional stability, the low power, horrendous engine fuel control systems and tricky ground handling of the early aircraft, and miss entirely the engineering achievement that not only allowed controlled flight, but enabled man to use his newly-gained aviation skill to turn the fragile aircraft into a weapon of war.

'A successful flight in one of these early aircraft can give the most intense feeling of personal satisfaction. In fact modern RAF fast jet types such as the Harrier and Jaguar do not require much more effort to fly, the complicity of the modern electronic systems contrasting nicely with the piloting qualities of the earlier machines.

The display pre-flight

'A display flight in the LF Mk VC starts with a look in the cockpit about 15 minutes before take-off to check all is in order and the switches are off. A walkaround the machine follows, particular notice being taken of cowlings, covers and control surfaces. Mind the antenna – a wire stretches from either side of the fuselage to the tailplane tip, creating a

'cheese cutter' barrier for the unsuspecting pilot not unlike that of the Avro Triplane! Back to the cockpit and strap in. A parachute is worn (partly as a seat cushion) and would be used in the unlikely event of an engine fire. Any other failure would cause an immediate landing back at Old Warden. In any event, for most of a typical display, the altitude would be too little to allow the parachute to open in time to save the pilot!

'After strap-in, a look around the cockpit confirms: ground flight switch to ground; full, free and correct movement of all controls; fuel on, brakes on (air pressure sufficient); radiator fully open; and the throttle set half an inch open and ready to start. A glance at the engineer gains his attention.

'"How many?"

'He looks away, appears deep in thought, contemplates the horizon, then the ground below.

'"Two-and-a-half!", is the considered reply.

'Accordingly, two-and-a-half shots of the primer are pumped into the carburettor. Stick hard back, clear all round.

'"CONTACT."

'The engineer checks that all around are ready and indeed clear.

'"CONTACT", he replies.

'Switches on, stick still hard back, expose starter and booster coil buttons, press both and hold. If all is well, one is rewarded with a cough as the engine barks into life and settles into a slow idle, sweeping a puff of smoke past the cockpit in the process. Check oil pressure – if it doesn't rise quickly then shut down. Wave away the ground power. As the engine warms, test for dead cut by turning each magneto off in turn. About five minutes is enough to warm the engine to the minimum temperature for running up. It is now a race against temperature and time to get airborne before the Merlin engine boils itself – the only severe disadvantage of the early marks over the later aircraft is the restricted cooling afforded by one solitary radiator positioned under the starboard wing.

'A wave of the finger signals the intention to run up. Two engineers run to the back of the machine and lie over the tailplane. Smoothly set 2000 rpm and cycle the prop from about 2000 to 1800 and back, ensuring warm oil in the constant speed mechanism. Each magneto is turned off then on in turn, noting the rpm drop (about 50) and lack of rough running. Set idle, wave away the chocks and taxy out. By now the temperature is rushing towards the red line, so take-off must not be delayed.

'Pre-take-off checks include: trim setting (both neutral as the Griffon and Merlin rotate in opposite directions, and on sound past advice, I set neutral rudder as foot forces can easily be held – if the trim is set in the wrong direction, however. . . !); throttle friction tight (see later); pitch fully forward (for take-off rpm); 'fuel on' contents checked; flaps up; gyros erect and set; gauges normal (temperature still rising); harness tight and locked; and hood closed or locked open (I prefer the former for take-off).

'I then check in with the tower, and on the appearance of a green light I am given permission to take-off. A quick look confirms all is clear. The brakes then come off, the stick is pulled hard back into the pit of my stomach and I open the throttle ever so slowly – too fast and the applied rudder will be insufficient to hold the fighter on the runway, or worse, it could tip onto its slender nose, wrecking a £30,000 propeller, and causing untold damage to the engine.

'Accelerating, right rudder is almost on the stop as 3000 rpm and eight inches boost are achieved. Ease forward on the stick to lower the nose, but not too much – the sight of grass through the front windscreen rather than engine and sky will be rapidly followed by the ploughing noise of the prop as it digs its way into the Old Warden turf. Not this time. The controls gain feel as flying speed is rapidly reached. She skips once or twice, whilst still accelerating, before a suggestion of rearward pressure on the stick raises the nose sufficiently to leave *terra firma*.

'Check the pitch rate immediately as the aircraft's very sensitive in pitch – particularly so in ground effect. A positive climb and altitude gain is confirmed, so change hands to raise the gear. It is now that a loose throttle friction nut will bite as the throttle will rapidly retard to the idle setting, causing an equally rapid 'changing of hands' by the pilot. With only two hands it is impossible to: a) guard the throttle; b) fly the aircraft; and c) tighten the throttle friction, so make a note of this essential pre-take-off check!

'Flying with the left hand, the gear is raised with the right. Watch for the lights on the instrument panel, as an undercarriage leg stuck in the mid position nicely blanks the radiator, rapidly accelerating the temperature rise in what is already an almost boiling system, with the obvious results. A red light marked 'UP' signals all is well.

'Ease the nose up to about 20°, throttle back to four inches boost and 2600 rpm, and then pause to collect your thoughts – a brief moment to reflect upon the fact that you are strapped into one of the most delightful flying machines ever built.

Flying the routine

'Back to work. Check the watch – two minutes to display time, which is just enough. Temperatures OK, with the all-important radiator gauge having fallen slightly since the gear was raised. Try the controls – pitch, yaw and roll OK. A quick look over the shoulder for the display line, and then a final scan of the gauges before running in and pulling the nose up to roll out at the top at about 2000 ft, with the nose aimed once again at the display line as it falls below the horizon. Down we go, faster and lower.

'Turbulence is felt as ground effect is reached. About 50 ft above the airfield on the first pass, with wings level at 250+ mph, and then pull gently back on the stick. Pitch stability is low in manoeuvre so light control pressures are required to prevent an overstress – only 3g is required. A force in excess of this will see me fail to achieve the required height. The horizon appears for the second time as the nose falls, so roll to wings level. Keep the g positive, as negative g will cut the engine due to fuel starvation – injection was not a standard feature on this particular mark!

'This manoeuvre is then repeated, but on the second pass along the crowd roll hard left into a climbing turn to show off the Spitfire VC's unique plan view. Roll off the bank and pull up into the first wingover, and at about 60° up use full aileron for a fast 420° roll, demonstrating the increased roll rate afforded by the clipped wings, before pulling the nose through and line up nicely for a 'top surface' pass – a euphemism for pulling into a hard turn past the tower, a manoeuvre loved by photographers, and one which has come to characterise all displays at Old Warden over the years owing to the airfield's curved display line. Pull up into a 420° roll and wing over, checking temperatures and pressures over the top as you peak out at about 1500 ft, with the speed down to perhaps as low as 70 mph.

'Pull down onto the display line and line up for the first barrel roll. Speed in excess of 200 mph, height again down to about 50 ft. Pull, check nose high, then roll. Complete the roll as the nose falls, but with lots of height in hand, check temperatures and time. Seven minutes for the full display from take-off is enough, as it's best to leave the audience wanting more. Line up pointing at the crowd line again, and depending on the direction, pull past the tower or roll and pull into a level turn.

'A good display should show all aspects of the aircraft – top, bottom and sides at least twice. If each manoeuvre can be made predictable, then the photographers are happy as they can anticipate when to take the picture. Capabilities should also be demonstrated. In the Shuttleworth Spitfire this equates to the fast roll rate of the clipped wing.

'The seven-minute mark is approaching. Line up for the last pass, low and fast. Pull up as crowd centre appears, then check, before rolling slowly, making sure to watch the negative g!

'With the display over it must be time to relax. Not yet, as the landing has to be made. Check temperature, throttle back, reduce speed and gain height. Turn down wind and check temperature – if too hot then fly around for a short while until cooler. Temperature will increase on finals as airflow is disrupted through the radiator by both gear and flaps, so it's better to start out with the gauges showing cooler readings. When satisfied – and below 140 mph – lower the gear. Make sure this is done in one smooth movement, as any hesitation will jam the lever, thus requiring negative g to release the hydraulic lock of the undercarriage leg on the undercarriage locks!

'The green light signals "DOWN", so drop the flap, open the hood and reduce speed to the stall. Light buffet at 65 mph is immediately followed by a gentle nose drop. "Over the hedge" speed will be 70 - 75 mph. Less would be inviting a stall on the approach, whilst more could see a possible overshoot of the landing runway. Neither are recommended! By now the final turn has commenced. Check your harness is tight and brake pressure sufficient. Final check of temperature, then concentrate on speed. Set maximum rpm in case of the need for a go around, then aim at the runway threshold and hold the speed. Over the hedge at 72 mph – perfect, close the throttle and ease to full back stick.

'With the rumbling sensation signalling touchdown, dance on the rudder pedals to prevent a ground loop as the aircraft slows. As a fast walking pace is achieved, raise the flaps – temperature is always in the back of the mind. Taxy in, weaving gently to see round the nose, and bring the machine to a halt with just enough margin left to set maximum rpm on the propeller lever and allow the pitch to move to fully course, the position preferred between flights. Check the magnetos and stop the engine before she boils. Switches off, fuel off, electrics off, brakes off. Unstrap, climb out and now we can relax, and smile!'

APPENDICES II

Spitfire Anatomy

As a member of the Ministry of Aircraft Production's Air Technical Publications department during World War 2, engineer S J Paine worked closely with Vickers-Armstrongs Supermarine in producing Air Publications – the official RAF manuals – for the Spitfire. Having documented all of its variants, including the Seafires, in 1945-46, Mr Paine wrote a detailed record of them for his own interest. It has never been published in book form until now – Ed.

This appendices deals exclusively with the story of the Spitfire and Seafire, that long line of fighters designed and built by Vickers-Armstrongs' Supermarine Works, and owing their ancestry to the monoplanes of Schneider Trophy fame, which of course were designed and built by the same firm.

The Spitfire was conceived in peace and developed in war, with a multiplicity of variants. When it retired, again in peace, it was still at the top of its class – where it had been throughout its ten years as a frontline military aircraft.

Throughout the war, but particularly through its most critical months, the name 'Spitfire' was a household word. Funds were started on almost any pre-text to raise £5000 to buy 'presentation' Spitfires, and many and varied were the names of people, organisations and towns which appeared on their fuselages.

This appendices gives the designations and the chronological order of appearance of all the types and variants of this versatile aircraft, and shows how development in other spheres – for example guns, gunsights, engines and accessories – were incorporated to the general betterment of the aircraft, and its performance. It shows, too, how the ever-changing demands of the Services were met, and how modifications were continually being made so that, at any given time, the aircraft being delivered to the RAF or Royal Navy were the last word in efficiency for their particular job.

Spitfire I

Spitfire I

In 1934, Vickers-Armstrongs Supermarine submitted a tender to the Air Ministry for a single-seat fighter to Specification F.37/34. A contract was placed, and in 1936 prototype K5054 completed its flight trials. Thus was the Spitfire born.

The fuselage was of stressed-skin construction, of oval cross-section, and tapered towards the rear. It had four main longerons and 15 channel-section frames numbered 5 to 19. The Alclad skin was riveted to the frames and stiffened between them by Z-section intercostals, which were riveted in place before the skin panels were attached to the frames. The fin was integral with the tail-end of the fuselage, which was detachable and bolted to the main portion by 52 bolts and four studs round a double frame.

The five forward frames, Nos 5 to 10, had the tops cut off and were thus of U-shape, the tops being joined by the top longerons. This portion of the fuselage housed the fuel tanks and, behind the tanks, the cockpit. Lateral members braced the fuselage at frame 5, which carried the fireproof bulkhead, and at frame 8. There was further bracing between frames 5 and 8 in the form of two detachable diagonal members extending across the tank bay and fitted after the bottom tank was in position.

Frame 11 braced the structure behind the cockpit seat and was the foremost of the complete frames shaping the fuselage.

Each wing was a separate stressed-skin elliptical structure. Each was, essentially, a single-spar wing, but each had an auxiliary spar. The mainspar and leading edge was constructed as a separate unit to which the main portion of the wing was afterwards assembled in a jig. The mainspar consisted of two square-section booms joined by a plate web. The booms were built up of square-section laminations, making the root ends almost solid, but tapering towards the tip first to channel-section, and finally to angle-section. The root end of this spar carried the pintle on which the retractable mainwheel pivoted.

Each wing was attached to the fuselage by the mainspar at the fireproof bulkhead, and by the auxiliary spar at frame 10. The auxiliary spar attachment used only one bolt, but the mainspar attachment used three bolts in the top boom and four in the bottom.

The control surfaces were of metal, but were fabric-covered.

The mainwheel units were cantilever structures which retracted into the undersurfaces of the wings. The retraction was effected hydraulically, in the first few aircraft by hand pump, but later by an engine-driven pump. The tailwheel was not retractable.

The span was 36 ft 10 in, and the overall length was 29 ft 10 in.

That, then, was the basic construction of the Spitfire, and it remained unchanged, except for local strengthening from time to time, throughout many increases in engine power and all-up weights, and more and more exacting duties during the war.

The Spitfire Mk I had eight 0.303 in Browning machine-guns, with 300 rounds in each ammunition box, a Merlin II or III engine, and initially a fixed pitch two-bladed wooden propeller – this was later changed to a de Havilland two-pitch/three-bladed unit, before the latter was converted to constant speed/variable-pitch in mid-1940. All of these things, individually the best in their own class, combined to make the Spitfire pre-eminent in performance. The policy of mounting the guns in the wings, outside the propeller disc, was to prove itself many times over in the years to follow.

By 1938, with rumblings on the Continent, the Spitfire was at last in production as a first-line military aircraft – the first aircraft reached No 19 Sqn at Duxford in August of that year. To be used as a day and night fighter, the Spitfire I had landing lamps, navigation and identification lamps, parachute flares for use in the event of a forced landing, oxygen supply and two-way radio. The landing lamps were under the wings and were retractable; they were lowered and retracted by the aircraft pneumatic system which also fired the guns. Also provided was an emergency gas system for lowering the mainwheels, using compressed carbon dioxide.

In order to record the aim of budding fighter pilots, a single-exposure gun-camera was installed in one wing and operated by the gun firing system. Later, this was superseded by a ciné camera, but in both cases the camera could be switched off while the actual guns were being fired. Also for use with the guns or camera was the reflector sight, which had a range scale, and a scale for the estimated span of the target.

The pilot was protected by a bullet-proof windscreen and armour plate behind his seat, and for his comfort there was cockpit heating. Ducts from this latter system also carried warm air to the guns to prevent them freezing up. The windscreen was kept clear of ice by a system which sprayed de-icing fluid over it.

The fuel was carried in two tanks, one above the other in front of the cockpit, each of which had a cock controlled from the cockpit. The bottom tank was covered with self-sealing material, and the combined capacity of the tanks was 85 gal.

The oil tank held 5.8 gal and was carried underneath the engine. Its bottom was shaped to the aircraft's nose contours so that it could remain uncowled and assist in the cooling of the oil.

The all-up weight of the Spitfire I was 5800 lbs, and the 1020 hp Merlin II or III engine gave it a top speed of 364 mph.

Spitfire II

Came the war, and more and more Spitfires were wanted, and they had to be able to fly faster and higher. Always the aim was to have the advantage of altitude. The Merlin XII was now installed, and the aircraft became the Mk II. This engine gave a higher rate of climb and a higher service ceiling – it also had cartridge instead of electrical starting.

As we gave our pilots armour protection, so did the enemy, and to pierce that armour heavier ammunition was required. A 20 mm Hispano gun, therefore, was installed in each wing in place of the two inboard 0.303 in Brownings. This different wing made the aircraft the Mk IIB, with armament of two 20 mm and four 0.303 in guns. Aircraft still fitted with eight 0.303 in guns were called Mk IIAs. The 20 mm guns had drum-type magazines holding 60 rounds each, the size of the drum necessitating the introduction of a blister in the top skin of the wing to clear the drum.

The all-up weight was now up to 6150 lbs, but the overall dimensions were the same, as was the maximum speed.

Spitfire III

The production of the Mk II merged fairly smoothly with that of the Mk I, but soon a new Rolls-Royce engine became available with a two-stage supercharger and increased power – the Merlin XX of 1240 bhp. The Spitfire designers then got to work on a new aircraft for this engine, and other features to enhance the fighter's already enviable reputation. The Mk III, as this new Spitfire was designated, had clipped wings and a retractable tailwheel unit. Also, the mainwheel units had extra fairings to cover the lower part of the wheel and tyre when retracted – this area had hitherto been unfaired.

The bullet-proof portion of the windscreen was fitted internally to obtain smoother lines externally, and with these improvements the top speed was increased to 385 mph.

A further improvement over the Mk II was the construction of the wings to provide for alternative armament of eight 0.303 in guns, four 0.303 in and two 20 mm, or four 20 mm guns. This type of wing became known as the 'universal' wing. The span had been reduced to 32 ft 7 in, and the aircraft gained a higher rate of roll for added manoeuvrability.

In all, some 90,000 man-hours were spent in the design of this type, but alas for the advantages of the Mk II, it did not go into quantity production. Only a few were made, but the improved features were subsequently incorporated in later marks.

Spitfire IV

This mark number was given to a type planned to incorporate a new Rolls-Royce engine not then in production. No aircraft went into production and the design was developed very much later an entirely new mark number.

Spitfire V

Spitfire VB

It was now 1941. Spitfire Is and IIs had played their part in the Battle of Britain, but air battles were now being fought higher and higher, and much farther afield. With high power at high altitude being demanded of fighter aircraft, Rolls-Royce answered the call with the Merlin 45 engine. This engine, in a still further improved airframe, gave us the Spitfire V, and still we had the advantage over the enemy. The airframe was virtually that of a Mk II, and the Merlin 45 or 46 engine was rated slightly lower than the Merlin XX, although it gave greater power at higher altitude. Thus, with normal, unclipped wings, the Spitfire V had enhanced performance near its ceiling. Actually, four close relatives of engine were used on this aircraft – they were the Mks 45, 46, 50 and 50A. The differences were within the engine and did not affect the aircraft.

Three variants of the Mk V were produced; the VA, having the same wings as the IIA; the VB, having the same wings as the IIB; and the VC, having the 'universal' wings of the Mk III. This latter wing provided a choice of armament to suit operational conditions, but it was generally found that the mixed armament – i.e. four 0.303 in and two 20 mm guns – was the more effective and the more popular with pilots. However, the change from one to the other could be effected quite quickly. In the Mk VC the 20 mm guns were belt-fed, the ammunition boxes holding 20 rounds per gun.

The capacity of the 0.303 in ammunition boxes also was increased to 350 rounds per gun. The Mk V, too, saw the introduction of extra armour protection, suitable armour plate being fitted above, below and in front of the 20 mm ammunition boxes, under the pilot's seat and in front of the coolant header tank. In addition, the cowling panel over the top fuel tank was made thicker to afford it some protection.

Sustained operations at high altitude meant exposure for long periods in the intense cold, so additional heating for the guns became necessary. The existing ducts for carrying the warm air to the guns reached only to the inboard gun bays, so additional pipes were laid to the outboard bays. The warm air was obtained by inserting a $1\frac{1}{4}$ in diameter pipe fore-and-aft through the engine exhaust stubs, the open end to the front and the aft end connected to further pipes passing inside the leading edge of the wing to the guns. This additional heating was fitted only on the Mks VB and VC.

Spitfire VB Trop

To facilitate rapid production, when speed of delivery to the RAF was vital, the fixed tailwheel unit was retained.

Up to now the fuel system and equipment had been the same for each mark, but with increased rate of climb and altitude came trouble with the fuel boiling as a result of the reduction in pressure without a reduction in temperature. Early Mk V aircraft had an electric pump in the bottom tank to assist flow at altitude, but retained a separate cock for each tank. Later aircraft omitted the cock on the top tank, with all the fuel cells being interconnected to function as one tank with a solitary cock.

Later aircraft of this mark – particularly those used overseas – had an improved fuel system which was 'pressurised' by the exhaust air from the aircraft's vacuum pump being directed into the top tank to raise the pressure on the fuel. This pressure was limited to $4\frac{1}{2}$ lbs per inch, but it improved the fuel flow and obviated the need for the electric pump. Also it reduced the tendency for the fuel to boil under certain conditions. This pressurisation came into action only at an altitude of approximately 25,000 ft as it was controlled by an aneroid valve set to that figure. It was not entirely advantageous, however, for under pressure the self-sealing property of the bottom tank was impaired – a cock was provided in the air pipeline so that the pressure could be exhausted and normal venting restored in the event of a bullet puncturing the bottom tank.

Another change in later aircraft was the deletion of the landing lamps, as the Spitfire V was no longer used as a nightfighter, and the introduction of metal ailerons in place of fabric-covered ones.

For operation in the Middle East, and other sandy or dusty places, the Mk V was provided with a tropical conversion set in the form of a filter in the air intake, and the pilot was given desert equipment for use in the event of his having to walk home from a forced landing. The air intake assembly comprised a duct with a shutter and a filter, all mounted on a panel interchangeable with the normal bottom engine cowling panel. The shutter admitted cold air, or warm air from around the engine, into the carburettor, but in both cases the air had to pass through the filter. The whole assembly gave the aircraft a very prominent 'chin'.

The pilot's desert equipment was carried in a container fitted behind his armoured head plate, and consisted of one half-gallon water tank and bottle, rations, a signal pistol and cartridges, canvas strips for ground signalling, a mirror and emergency tools. If the pilot had a long walk in front of him, he could strap the container on his back.

With operations on widely different fronts, there came a demand for aircraft with different full-throttle heights so that the maximum efficiency could be obtained at the appropriate level of combat. Three marks of Merlin engine – the 45, 50 and 55 – were altered by cropping the supercharger impeller to a smaller diameter, and thus reducing the full-throttle height, and, incidentally, changing their nomenclature to 45M, 50M and 55M respectively. These engines fitted to the Spitfire V gave rise to the Low Altitude (LF) variant, as opposed to the earlier Mk Vs, which were designated with a single F. Variants of this mark now became F VA, F VB, F VC, LF VA, LF VB and LF VC.

Spitfire VB (Aboukir filter)

Still more versatility, however, was required of this aircraft. Battle fronts were becoming farther from base with the advent of tactical and strategic bombing, and greater distances had to be flown before contact was made with the enemy. Greater range, therefore, was necessary if the fuel tanks were not to run dry in the height of battle. The aircraft wanted more fuel, but did not want the tank it was carried in. Jettisonable overload tanks were therefore introduced, which were later nicknamed 'drop tanks', in true American terminology. At first, 30 gal of extra fuel were carried in a blister-shaped tank underneath the fuselage.

A cock and feed line were provided, and also means of dropping the tank when empty so as not to impair the aircraft's performance. Subsequently, a 90 gal tank of similar shape was carried and dropped in the same way.

The jettison mechanism was quite simple, consisting of two shallow hooks on the fuselage, into which corresponding fittings on the tank engaged, and a grooved pin which passed into the fuselage to be engaged by a spring-loaded keyhole fitting operated by the pilot. The tank was prevented from sliding along the underside of the fuselage in the slipstream by two 'stop' hooks at the rear, which forced the front of the tank to drop on being jettisoned, and to separate from the aircraft.

When it was required to transport Spitfires to the Middle East in 1941/42 at short notice, and ships were having difficulty in making the trip both intact and in time, it was decided to fly some aircraft there under their own power. Accordingly, an outsize drop tank was made – it held 170 gal, and when fitted on the aircraft allowed very little ground clearance. In addition, an extra tank holding 29 gal was installed in the rear of the fuselage. These two tanks were for ferrying purposes only, and necessitated an oil tank of twice the normal size – this was fitted in place of the normal oil tank. Another provision for long-range ferrying was the installation of an extra oxygen bottle.

With such an overload it was necessary to remove all armament in order to keep the all-up weight down to a reasonable figure. In any case, when fitted with a drop tank the aircraft was restricted to straight and level flying as much as possible.

Having been used for high-level and low-level fighting, the Spitfire V was now required to take part in ground strafing too, and to this end it was arranged for a bomb to be carried under the fuselage. The adapter was T-shaped and fitted into the drop tank fittings. The necessary wiring was installed, and the release switch was housed in the throttle lever under the pilot's thumb.

The Mk V really was the first true 'multi-role' Spitfire, and as such was built in considerable numbers both for the RAF and a number Allied air forces including the RAAF, USAAF and Soviet Air Forces. It was used for patrolling and fighting over varied distances, at all heights, and in temperate and tropical zones. Its adaptability and usefulness made it a highly valued tool in the fight against the enemy across the globe.

Early Photo Reconnaissance Marks

Spitfire PR IV

The Photographic Reconnaissance Units converted a number of fighter aircraft to carry various F24, F8 or F52 camera installations in the fuselage and in the wings. There were two main Spitfire types at this stage, and they were given their own series of photographic reconnaissance mark numbers.

The PR Mk IV and PR Mk VII were both conversions from the F Mk V. The PR Mk IV had new wings without guns, but the whole of the leading edge of each wing forward of the mainspar formed a fuel tank of approximately 66 gal capacity. To provide the necessary oil to go with this fuel, a tank holding 18 gal was installed in the port wing. This gave great range, but meant that having obtained his photographs, the pilot had to streak for home and not invite combat.

The PR Mk VII had normal wings, with armament depending on the type of fighter converted, but only the 0.303 in guns were carried. Some extra fuel was carried in a 29 gal tank in the rear of the fuselage. This meant shorter range than the PR Mk IV, but gave the pilot a chance to fight his way home should he be intercepted.

The PR IV had three types of camera installation – the first provided two F8 20 in focal length cameras mounted vertically and facing through windows in the bottom of the fuselage, whilst the second provided two F24 14 in cameras mounted vertically and one F24 8 in, or 14 in, mounted obliquely and facing through a window in the port side of the fuselage. The third type of installation provided a single F52 36 in focal length camera mounted vertically.

The vertical cameras of the first two installations were 'fanned' at approximately 20° to each other to increase the field of view, but still maintained an overlap on the plates.

The installation in the PR VII provided two F24 cameras of different focal lengths mounted vertically, but not 'fanned', and an F24 8 in or 14 in mounted obliquely and facing through a window in either the port or starboard side of the fuselage.

The windows in the bottom of the fuselage were covered with spring-loaded flaps to exclude dirt and mud during take-off, but the flaps could afterwards be jettisoned by the pilot. In some installations the cameras were heated electrically by muffs and sleeves, and in others by either a box or canvas bag enclosing the cameras and supplied with hot air from behind the radiator under the starboard wing.

The all-up weights of these two PR aircraft were slightly higher than the F Mk V, at 7050 lb, but the PR IV, with its clean leading edge, showed an increase in maximum speed to 382 mph.

Later some Spitfire Vs were converted for low-altitude photographic reconnaissance by the installation of the Merlin 32 engine. The only extra fuel provided for this type was carried in a 30 gal drop tank – otherwise these aircraft were similar to the PR VII, and were designated PR XIII. All armed PR aircraft had bulletproof windscreens and retained the camouflage finish, but the PR IV, and subsequent unarmed PR types, had rounded windscreens and were painted all over with PR blue.

It should be stated at this stage that the system of allocating mark numbers changed from time to time, so that in some instances there appear duplications, while at other times there appear gaps.

Early Naval Marks

Also casting covetous eyes on the Spitfire was the Royal Navy, and in 1941 a Spitfire V was fitted with a deck arrestor hook and was landed on an aircraft carrier. This became the first of many Seafires, and was designated Seafire IB. The name retained the 'fire' part of Spitfire, whilst the 'Sea' prefix came from the standard practice of naming naval conversions of land-based aircraft. The mark number was obvious, and the 'B' came from it being a conversion of the Spitfire VB, with the mixed-armament wing and the Merlin 45 or 46 engine.

The arrestor hook was carried at the apex of an A-shaped tubular frame, and was housed under the rear end of the fuselage. The two legs of the frame were hinged near frame 15, where the structure was reinforced, and the frame had a curved fairing to maintain the fuselage shape during flight. When the hook and frame were retracted, only the hook itself projected below the fuselage profile. The hook was held in the up position by a spring-loaded snap gear released from the cockpit, and was pushed and held down by a spring-loaded jack pivoted on the hook frame and on the fuselage. The interior of the fuselage was sealed from the hook frame housing by a closing plate fastened to the frames and to the longerons.

To provide a means of slinging the complete aircraft on a crane, spigots were fitted on each side of the fuselage at the engine bulkhead, and at frame 16 in the rear portion of the fuselage. Reinforcing plates were introduced under the skin at these points to provide the extra strength required.

The all-up weight of the Seafire IB was 6700 lb, and the man-hours expended on it were 10,000 in design and 18,000 in jigs and tools.

Inevitably Seafires developed independently, and the next of this basic type had the 'universal' wings of the Spitfire VC. This, together with the introduction of catapult spools, made it the Seafire IIC. With provision for catapulting, extra strength was needed, and this was provided by having an extra strong fuselage frame at the catapult spool positions, frames 9 and 16, and reinforcement at frame 10.

Internal strengthening was also provided in the main portions of the longerons and around the radio compartment door. Since the rear catapult spools were conveniently placed as rear slinging spigots, the latter were subsequently deleted. Still later, both front and rear catapult spools were made detachable.

For occasions when a catapult was not available, and conditions were not suitable for a normal take-off, some early Seafires were provided with facilities for rocket-assisted take-off. In this instance two 4 in rockets were housed in a carrier and mounted on the wing close to the fuselage on each side of the aircraft. They were fired by the pilot and lifted the aircraft off after a very short run. The carriers were jettisoned after take-off.

To suit climatic conditions, the Seafires could have either the temperate or tropical air intake installations of the Spitfire V.

In due course the Navy also became particular about optimum performance at the operational altitude of the moment, so some Mk IIC aircraft were fitted with a Merlin 32 engine and a four-bladed propeller. This was the only change in the aircraft, but it altered the designation to Seafire L IIC. From this stage onwards, all Seafires had four-bladed propellers.

A further variation embodied in the L IIC was the installation of two F24 cameras in the fuselage, on vertical and one oblique. The cameras could be of various focal lengths, similar to those on the Spitfire PR VII, and the oblique camera could be mounted to face to port or starboard as desired. The camera windows were similar to those in the Spitfire PR types. Since this was not quite a PR type, but was used for fighter recce duties, it was called the FR IIC.

The all-up weight of each of these Mk II variants

was 7300 lb. Comparatively few man-hours were spent in design (4000), but many more (40,000) were expended on the jig and tool side of the development

Spitfire VI

Spitfire VI

In 1941 it was apparent that increased performance at extreme altitude was essential. Although Spitfires could operate at 40,000 ft, the pilot's reactions were laboured and slow, and he could not get the best out of the aircraft. Vickers Supermarine staff soon produced a pressure-cabin version of the Spitfire VB, and gave the pilot the advantage of cockpit conditions of 30,000 ft at an altitude of 40,000 ft. This was effected by installing a Merlin 47 engine, which had an extra accessory drive, and using a Marshall blower to pass air into the cockpit and maintain therein a pressure of some 2 lb/in^2 above the surrounding atmospheric pressure. The air was retained in the 'cabin' by two extra bulkheads, one in front of and one behind the cockpit, and by the sealing of all structural joints and so on with sealing compound on assembly. Control runs, pipes and cables were provided with pressure-tight glands, fixed or flexible according to the type of control, where they passed through the bulkheads.

The incoming air was filtered at its entry into the blower and conveyed along the starboard side of the engine and airframe into the fuselage. Inside the cockpit the air was diverted by small perforated pipes to the hood and windscreen panels, thus using the pressurising air to prevent misting on the canopy panels.

The pressure in the cockpit was controlled by a manually-operated valve, but the supply of air was continuous. Later aircraft had an automatic valve which allowed the pressure to build up automatically with altitude. A cockpit altimeter indicated the effective height of the cockpit, and warning lamps showed if the pressure dropped by more than 1 lb/in^2.

Spitfire VI

Other differences in this aircraft were the extended wingtips, which increased the span to 40 ft 2 in, and slightly reduced the wing loading, plus a detachable, non-sliding, hood. This latter feature saved time which would have been spent in designing an effective means of sealing the cockpit hood and door slides. The hood was located by pegs and locked down before take-off, and could not be moved by the pilot (except for jettisoning) before landing was completed. This soon made the type unpopular, as it was usual to taxy, take-off and land with the sliding hood open. Another externally recognisable feature was the introduction of the four-bladed propeller.

The aim to provide comfort for the pilot at extreme altitude was more than successful: whereas he had previously needed heated clothing at 40,000 ft, in the Mk VI it was possible to fly at that altitude in shirt-sleeves owing to the warming effect of the slightly compressed incoming air. On offensive operations over enemy territory, however, shirtsleeves were not the most practical wear, so a means of bypassing the air from the blower when not required was duly requested.

Another objection to the continuous supply of air was that it brought with it into the cockpit the noise of the blower and drive. Actually, the means of overcoming this nuisance was not incorporated in this aircraft, but was introduced in later marks. In other aspects the aircraft was similar to the Spitfire VB, except that the tube and controls for the parachute flare were omitted, and no bombs could be carried.

The man-hours expended on this type were 14,000 in design and 50,000 in jigs and tools. The all-up weight was 6750 lb.

Spitfire VII and VIII

Spitfire HF VII

By 1942 Rolls-Royce had produced a still bigger and better engine which had a two-speed, two-stage supercharger. This engine was the Merlin 60 and 70 series, which had an increased full-throttle height, with greater power at that altitude - the engine output was up to 1400 bhp. It also operated at higher boost – 12 lb/in^2, with 15 lb/in^2 for combat. This was later increased still further to 18 lb/in^2. There were several variations of the new engine, and aircraft were designated according to the engine installed, as follows:
Merlin 61 and 64 (SU carburettor) – F Mk VII
Merlin 71 (Injection carburettor) – HF Mk VII
Merlin 61, 63, 63A (SU carburettor) – F Mk VIII
Merlin 66 (Injection carburettor) – LF Mk VIII
Merlin 70 (Injection carburettor) – HF Mk VIII
The L and F prefixes denoted low- or high-altitude characteristics.

Two aircraft types were scheduled to incorporate the new engine – the Spitfires Mk VII and Mk VIII.

Spitfire VII

Both types had strengthened engine mountings, fuselage and undercarriage struts. Both types also had the extended wingtips of the Mk VI, and a small 12 gal fuel tank mounted in each wing leading edge. These marks also incorporated the retractable tailwheel unit of the Spitfire III. The larger protuberance of engine necessitated some compensating area at the rear, and on these and subsequent marks a larger rudder and trimming tab were fitted.

Spitfire VIII

The great difference between these two types was that the Mk VII had a pressure cabin along the same lines as the Mk VI.

So good was the new engine that time for full development and production of the Mks VII and VIII could ill be spared at this stage, and as an interim measure, in order to take rapid advantage of the engine's power, it was introduced into the Mk VC airframe. The resulting aircraft was called Mk IX.

Spitfire IX

Spitfire F IXC

As stated above, the Mk IX was produced as an interim version. Alterations necessary to the Mk VC airframe included the strengthening of the fuselage and undercarriage, and revision of the radiator system. The geometry of the undercarriage was altered slightly for centre of gravity considerations, and the intercooler on the Merlin 61 engine necessitated a radiator. The new layout for the radiators put a main coolant radiator and the intercooler radiator under the starboard wing, and a main coolant radiator and the oil cooler under the port wing. In this way the cooling system was split, and was symmetrical along each side of the engine and airframe. The intercooler radiator and the oil cooler were each mounted alongside the accompanying main radiator in the same fairing. With the new radiator layout was introduced automatic adjustment of the radiator flaps of earlier aircraft. The automatic adjustment was governed by a thermostat in the main cooling system, and a pneumatic jack connected to the flaps.

Although it was the Mk VC that was converted, the armament was fixed at two 20 mm and four 0.303 in guns. This armament now became standard for this type of wing. The gun heating system, however, underwent a change. Now that there was a radiator under each wing, there was no need to carry the ducts across the fuselage as for the Mk V and other types. On this aircraft, the system was the same in each wing, a duct carrying air from the rear of the radiator outboard and forward in the wing, with a small branch pipe to the side of each individual gun. A baffle was made outboard of the guns to keep the warm air within bounds.

The rapid conversion meant that the Mk IX was in service before either the Mk VII or VIII and, with an all-up weight of 7300 lb, it had a speed of 410 mph. The larger engine gave it an overall length of 31 ft (13 in longer than the Mk V). Later Mk IXs also had to the larger rudder of the Mk VII.

This mark had such a good performance, and became so popular, that many more than the planned number were eventually produced. The type had a long an useful life, so much so that several variants made their bow. First, the Mk IX had either a Merlin 61, 63 or 63A, and here again the different numbers meant only slight differences in the engine. For optimum speed at lower altitude the Merlin 66 was introduced, producing the LF Mk IX, and for optimum speed at higher altitude the installation of the Merlin 70 gave the HF Mk IX.

Both the Merlin 66 and 70 had the Bendix Stromberg injection type carburettor instead of the normal gravity-feed carburettor, and also different supercharger gear and propeller reduction gear ratios. These two engines also had a booster pump in the fuel system, which took the form of a hand pump on early aircraft but was later electrified.

The supercharger gear change on the Merlin 61 series was effected automatically at the appropriate altitude, depending on the setting of the switch, and was governed by an aneroid valve. This valve caused an electro-pneumatic valve to admit or cut off the supply of compressed air to the supercharger ram.

To obviate the need for a tropical air intake conversion set, a new air intake assembly which included a filter was introduced. A shutter in the forward-facing intake could be operated by the pilot to allow air to pass straight through to the carburettor, or to divert the air through the filter before it entered the carburettor. The duct and filter unit fitted snugly under the engine, and was enclosed by the bottom cowling panel. There were three types of air intake assembly used in the life of the Mk IX, all of which enabled the aircraft to operate in temperate or tropical conditions without the need to change any accessories.

The Mk IX was later chosen to be the first in the range to carry 0.5 in Browning guns. The 'universal' wing had two 20 mm gun bays, but only the inboard one was used when the mixed armament was carried. This 20 mm weapon was now moved to the outboard bay, and the 0.5 in Browning was installed in the inboard bay. The 0.303 in guns were deleted, leaving the new armament as two 20 mm and two 0.5 in guns. The ammunition boxes for the 0.5 in guns each held 25 rounds. With this installation, the gun heating ducts were cut off just inboard of the 0.5 in gun and the outboard sections removed. The change in armament meant a change in nomenclature, and the suffix E was added to the mark number. As the 0.5 in guns were fitted only to LF and HF aircraft, the new list of variants was F IX, LF IX, LF IXE, HF IX and HF IXE.

A further improvement in connection with the armament was the introduction on later Mk IXs of the Gyro gunsight. This eliminated a good deal of the human element when it came to aiming the guns, although it added quite a lot more 'furniture' to an already very full cockpit. There were two types of installation, although in both of them the sight was so near to the pilot's face that a protective pad was provided to cover the front of the instrument in the event of a crash landing.

The versatility of this aircraft was still not exhausted, however, and in addition to a Mk V-type drop tank or bomb, the Mk IX could carry up a 250 lb bomb under each wing at the 20 mm gun position. Normally these wing bombs were released electro-mechanically, but in case this method failed a Bowden cable mechanical release was also provided.

A total of 43,800 man-hours went into the design work on this major mark, and jigs and tools accounted for 30,000. The larger engine had raised the all-up weight to 7500 lb.

Late Photo Reconnaissance Marks

Spitfire PR XI

High speed at high altitude was just the thing the photographic reconnaissance units required, and they quickly seized on the qualities of the Spitfire IX due to its ability showing a clean pair of heels to an inquisitive enemy. The job of the PR pilot was to get the photographs and get home – no heroic combats for him. Accordingly, some Mk IX aircraft were converted to carry extra fuel and F24 cameras. For the extra fuel needed, wings similar to those on the PR IV were fitted, having leading-edge tanks holding 66 gal each. One difference was that the cocks at the inboard ends of the tanks were remotely-controlled by the pilot.

Although the main fuel tanks were pressurised as in the Mk IX, these leading-edge tanks were not, although the vents at the outboard ends each had a ball valve to prevent loss of fuel during aerobatics. Another difference in the wing of the PR Mk XI, as this version was now called, was the carriage of desert equipment, similar to that on earlier tropical aircraft, in the undersurface of the starboard wing.

Since no air combat was to be indulged in, the bullet-proof windscreen was deleted in favour of a plain, curved, windscreen. This and the clean leading edge of the wings, together with the faired-in retractable tailwheel, gave the aircraft very smooth lines, and as a consequence there was an increase of 5 mph in speed over a comparable Mk IX. The retractable tailwheel now began to be incorporated in all new marks, although it was raised and lowered hydraulically, as the carbon dioxide system for lowering the mainwheels did not lower the tailwheel.

The camera installations for this latest PR variant were the same as for the PR IV - two 'fanned' F8 20 in vertical cameras, or two 'fanned' F24 vertical and one oblique, or one F52 36 in vertical. Later PR XIs had a 'universal' installation whereby any of three sets of cameras could quickly be interchanged, using the same bearers in the aircraft. These sets were comprised either two fanned F52 36 in vertical; two fanned F8 20 in or F52 20 in vertical; two fanned F24 vertical; or one F24 oblique facing to port. This last variant was identical with the earlier combinations of F24s.

With this 'universal' installation, an improved method of heating was introduced. This consisted of ducts leading from behind the radiator in each mainplane to a heater box in the cockpit. A single duct led aft from this box, and was divided into three, one arm going to each of the vertical and oblique camera apertures. A plywood bulkhead was added to frame 15 to prevent the warm air from dissipating along the fuselage. The camera controls were similar to those for other installations.

To clear the cameras in the fuselage, the elevator and rudder control cables had to be guided round pulleys, and in place of the 15 cwt duplicated cables of earlier types, the Mk XI had single 20 cwt cables. Later, these were further strengthened to 25 cwt.

Still later PR XIs also had an F24 5 in camera in each wing. They were fitted just outboard of the wheel-well in a blister attached to the undersurface. The camera, its mounting, camera motor and blister were all mounted on a detachable panel which fitted between wing ribs 9 and 12. The lens faced outboard 10° from the vertical, and was heated by warm air conveyed from behind the radiator to the interior of the housing formed by the panel and the filled-in adjacent ribs. For these wing cameras, an extra control unit was installed in the cockpit.

Apart from having no armament, a longer nose and the PR blue colouring, another recognisable feature of later PR XIs was the larger rudder of the Mk VII. The all-up weight of the PR XI was 7800 lbs.

Spitfire XII

Spitfire F XIIC

At about the time of the Spitfire IX, Rolls-Royce introduced the first of the Griffon series engines. This powerplant, the Griffon III, was installed in a Spitfire VC airframe and, with a few other changes, identified the Spitfire XII. The new engine was unlike the Merlin series in several ways: it had larger-diameter cylinders, making the cylinder blocks bigger; its direction of rotation was left-hand tractor against the right-hand tractor of the Merlins; and it was designed to be used with a girder-type engine mounting and not the tubular type hitherto used for Merlin engines. Another departure in the design of this engine was the elimination of accessories from the engine itself, and the provision of a single coupling and shaft for driving an accessory gearbox, separate from the engine and mounted on the fireproof bulkhead.

The Griffon was larger and its power output was greater (1500 hp), but it only had a single-stage supercharger, and therefore no intercooler. In spite of this it was longer than the Merlin 61 series, and with a very long spinner, and a larger rudder on the airframe, it made the length of this new mark 31 ft 10 in. The new rudder was similar to that used on later PR XIs.

The Mk XII had an improved maximum speed at low altitude, and to increase manoeuvrability the wings were clipped like to those on the Mk III. This reduced the span but increased the rate of roll.

With the lengthening of the nose, there came a deterioration in the pilot's view forward, so to minimise this the top cowling panel was 'blistered' to fit over the cylinder blocks and lie snugly in the vee between them.

Another change necessitated by the introduction of the new engine was the removal of the oil tank from under the powerplant, on account of the larger crankcase of the Griffon, and its repositioning behind the fireproof bulkhead in front of the top main fuel tank. This meant a sacrifice of some 10-11 gal in the capacity of the top main fuel tank. This, and the introduction – after the first few – of the retractable tailwheel, were the only modifications made to the VC airframe.

Design work on the Mk XII accounted for 27,000 man-hours, while 16,000 were expended on jigs and tools. The all-up weight was 7300 lbs.

Oddities

In 1942 several one-offs types were produced in the form of two Spitfires on floats (shades of the Schneider Trophy), and a PR IX. The floatplanes carried their floats on well-faired vertical stubs just outboard of the positions usually occupied by the undercarriage struts. One aircraft was converted from a Mk V, the other from a Mk IX, and both had an extra fin fitted underneath the normal tail unit, although the Mk IX had a different fin and rudder profile. The PR IX was simply the fighter fitted with two F24 cameras, and it was later developed into the PR Mk XI.

More Seafires

During the progress work carried out on Spitfires, those responsible for the naval side of fighter aircraft had not been idle. Early in 1942 the next step from the Seafire FR IIC was to provide folding wings to facilitate hangar stowage, deck ranging and so on aboard aircraft carriers. The Navy set the dimensional limits, and the aircraft (with wings folded) had to be within those limits. The result was that the Seafire wings were made to fold just inboard of the 20 mm guns. Each hinge was formed at the top boom of the front spar and at the rear spar; the locking point was at the bottom of the front spar, where a tapered bolt was screwed into appropriate mating lugs. Fairing doors were provided in the top skin to cover gaps in the fold line at the hinges, and these and the main bolt were locked by means of pins operated by cable from a single lever in the wheel bay. Locating spigots were provided at the leading edge, front spar and trailing edge, and the gun heating ducts were provided with a felt butt joint at the fold.

The wings folded upwards and over to nearly 30° beyond the vertical, and were held in that position by telescopic struts connected to the folding portions and to the root end fixed portions. To keep within the vertical dimension the wingtips were arranged to fold down in a similar manner, the hinge in this case being at the bottom boom of the front spar and at the rear spar. A small strut, stowed inside the adjacent portion of the wing, was fitted between the separated locking lugs of the top boom to hold the folded wingtip rigid.

The overall dimensions with wings folded were 13 ft 4 in wide and 13 ft 6 in high. The folding and spreading operations were carried out manually by a party of five men. Another feature of the wing was the 20 mm ammunition box, which could be removed from underneath when loading with wings spread, or hinged outwards from the top for loading with the wings folded.

The folding wings made this aircraft the Seafire Mk III, but another difference from the F IIC was the Merlin 55 engine. Later, the fitment of the Merlin 55M – with a cropped impeller again – resulted in the LF Mk III for low-altitude operations. Still later, the camera installation of the FR IIC, (one vertical and one oblique F24) was introduced into the LF Mk III, which became the FR Mk III, with the only difference being that one camera was carried in the latter type.

Late Spitfire Mk VIIs and VIIIs

1943 saw the full development of the Mks VII and VIII. These two aircraft were similar except that the Mk VII had a pressure cabin which necessitated the sealing of all structural joints, and the provision of glands for the moving controls. The seals and glands were an improvement on those used in the Mk VI, and in addition a 'spill' valve was provided to bypass the air from the blower and prevent it entering the cockpit when it was not required. Because the detachable hood of the Mk VI had been so unpopular, a pressurised sliding hood was designed for the Mk VII, so that it could open and shut like a normal hood, be sealed as part of the pressure cabin, and also be jettisoned in an emergency. This was achieved by having an inflatable tube round the edge of the hood, and hinged sides to the fuselage slides. Normally, the hood slid fore-and-aft in the usual manner, but when the cabin was being pressurised some of the air was diverted to the tube and inflated in its housing to render the joints pressure-tight.

If it became necessary to jettison the hood, a spring-loaded mechanism could be operated to push the hinged slides and allow the hood to be elbowed out and up into the slipstream, free of the aircraft. The jettison mechanism was mounted on the back of frame 11, behind the pilot, and was operated by a coiled spring which had to be wound up and set before flight. The mechanism was released by the pilot pulling on a knob in the cockpit, but in the event of a mishap it could be released from outside by means of a ring and cable attached to the normal control, and passing just through the fuselage skin.

From the blower to the spill valve, the air line was similar to that on the Mk VI, but in the case of the Mk VII the air to the hood tube was tapped off the main line just aft of the blower, and led separately to a cock on the port side of the cockpit. From the cock, one pipe led to the hood tube, and another to the outside atmosphere so that the hood could be sealed, or not, as required.

The pressure in the cabin was built up with increased altitude by means of an automatic valve on the rear pressure bulkhead, and could be maintained at $2^{1}/_{2}$ lb/in^{2} above the surrounding atmosphere pressure. This gave cockpit conditions of approximately 10,000 ft lower than the true altitude.

Another feature of the hood and cabin top on Mk VII aircraft was the fact that the windscreen, hood and window aft of the pilot were double-glazed, having an air space between the inner and outer panels. This trapped air was kept dry, to avoid misting, by being kept in contact with crystalline silica-gel. These crystals were kept in a container behind the pilot, the container being connected to the interspaces of the windscreen and window by small tubes. The hood itself had its own compartment containing crystals, which were blue when dry, but when they absorbed moisture they turned pink – their condition could be easily observed by groundcrews after a sortie, and duly changed when necessary.

As with the earlier marks, alternative engines were installed in the Mk VII and VIII airframes to provide aircraft for different altitudes. The Merlin 61 or 64 gave us the F VII, and the Merlin 71 the HF VII. Being a pressure cabin aircraft, there was no call for an LF version of the Mk VII. In fact, very few HF VIIs were produced either.

In the case of the Mk VIII, the Merlin 61, 63 or 63A gave us the F VIII, the Merlin 66 the LF VIII and the Merlin 70 the HF VIII. The variants of the Mk VIII were the same as those for the Mk IX, but the only differences in the engines for the Mk VII was the provision of the drive for the cabin blower.

Spitfire LF VIIIC

The air intake assembly on the Mk VIII was the same as that for the Mk IX, incorporating a filter which could be bypassed if required, but the Mk VII had the older direct-entry type intake without a filter.

All other features, as follows, were the same on both Mks VII and VIII. The fuel system suffered its first major change from earlier marks in that the combined contents of the two main tanks was increased to 96 gal by shaping the tanks to fit more snugly into the corners and crevices in the tank bay. The bottom tank was of welded light-alloy, and the top tank was of flexible, self-sealing material.

Also, a $12^{1}/_{2}$ gal tank was introduced into each leading edge near the root end. These tanks were detachable and also of flexible, self-sealing material, unlike the leading-edge tanks of the PR types, which were formed in the actual wing structure. The fuel in the wing tanks was transferred, when required, to the top main tank by air from the exhaust side of the aircraft vacuum pump being directed into the tanks. The pressure of this air was approximately $4^{1}/_{2}$ lb/in^{2}, and each tank could be selected for transfer in its turn by means of a plunger-type valve mounted on the fireproof bulkhead, and operated by the pilot. The transfer of fuel from each tank took about two minutes, and was not to be made, of course, until the drop tank had been emptied and jettisoned, and a suitable quantity used from the main tanks.

The system was pressurised as for earlier systems, and a booster pump was installed for use with the Merlin 70 or 71 engines, which had Bendix Stromberg carburettors.

The oil tank was carried in the usual place under the engine, but was now larger and was totally enclosed by the bottom engine cowling panel. A few early Mk VIIs, however, were built with the oil tank in the fuselage behind the rear pressure bulkhead. All were subsequently modified.

The cooling system, the layout of the radiators, and the gun heating system, was the same as for the Mk IX.

Although the all-up weight of the Mk VII was 7900 lb and the Mk VIII 7750 lb, their speed was equal to that of the lighter Mk IX – namely 410 mph – thanks to the higher performance Merlin engines, plus more streamlined aerodynamics. The extended wingtips put the span up to 40 ft 2 in, and the overall length was 31 ft 9 in. The first few aircraft had the original elliptical rudder, but this was superseded by the larger rudder of the Mk XII and the PR XI.

Man-hours expended on design in connection with the Mk VII totalled 86,000, while the Mk VIII needed 25,000. Jigs and tools, on the other hand, absorbed 250,000 man-hours for the Mk VIII and 150,000 for the Mk VII.

Large numbers of the Mk VIIIs were produced, with most being used almost exclusively overseas in the Middle East, India, Burma and Australia.

Spitfire PR Mk X

Spitfire PR X

In 1944, the photographic reconnaissance units thought that they would like a pressure-cabin aircraft for high-altitude operations, and they therefore requested a PR version of the Mk VII. Only a few were made, as the aim was merely to gain experience in pressure-cabin operation for a later, more powerful, version of the aircraft which was on the stocks.

The variant finally emerged as an F Mk VII (Merlin 64) fitted with the wings and camera installation of the PR XI – it was called PR Mk X. An addition to the fuel system was the introduction of immersed electric pumps into the leading-edge tanks. The fuel in these tanks was not pressurised or transferred, but fed direct to the carburettor through independent cocks. Each leading-edge tank had its own contents gauge in the cockpit.

Another slight difference was the repositioning of the aneroid vent, and other drains, in the rear of the fuselage behind the camera apertures in order to avoid drips of oil and so on being blown on to the camera windows.

Single 25 cwt cables were used for the elevator and rudder controls, and the camera installation was that of the PR XI. Additional access doors were provided in the fuselage to facilitate the installation and removal of the cameras. Wing cameras were not fitted to this mark.

In addition to the leading edge tanks, a 90 gal drop tank could be carried, and to cope with the increased, range three oxygen bottles were installed in place of the one in the Mk VII. These bottles were housed behind the pilot and within the pressure-cabin. This aircraft had the 31 ft 9 in overall length of the Mk VII, but only the 36 ft 10 in span of the PR XI. Its all-up weight was 7000 lb.

Spitfire XIV

With the exception of the Mk XII, all Spitfires had hitherto been powered by Merlin engines. Although the excellent Merlin was by no means becoming second-rate, a still more powerful powerplant had been perfected by Rolls-Royce for use mainly with single-engined aircraft. This engine, called the Griffon, had bigger cylinders than the Merlin, and consequently had larger overall dimensions. The exterior was kept clear of accessories, however, by the provision of a single coupling and shaft which drove an accessory gearbox separate from the engine and mounted on the fireproof bulkhead. There were two series of Griffon engine: the earlier one had a two-speed single-stage supercharger and was fitted to the Spitfire XII; while the later series had a two-speed two-stage supercharger, necessitating an intercooling system similar to that of the later Merlin engines.

Supermarine built an airframe to accommodate one of these later-series engines, designated the Griffon 65, which was rated to develop up to 2000 hp. As the system of mark numbering was now to run consecutively whether the type was an RAF fighter, Fleet Air Arm Seafire or PR aeroplane, this new aircraft was called the F Mk XIV. The appreciably increased thrust of the Griffon meant a propeller with greater diameter had to be fitted to absorb the power, but as a larger-diameter four-bladed propeller was out of the question for the Spitfire, owing to its already small ground clearance, Rotol produced a five-bladed constant-speed propeller instead. The alternative solution of contra-rotating propellers was still having teething troubles at this time, and was not perfected sufficiently to incorporate in Service aircraft.

The airframe of the Mk XIV was essentially a strengthened and modified Mk VIII, but in view of the still longer nose, the fin and rudder area had to increase still further. In this instance, for the first time the fin itself was enlarged, and the whole fin and rudder outline improved to encompass the larger area. The trimming tab on the rudder was also arranged to provide balance action to ease the load on the rudder bar. None of these changes upset the graceful lines of the well-known Spitfire, however. In fact, the increased length enhanced its beauty, and the symmetry of the five-bladed propeller added to the impression of power already gained by its predecessors.

The armament on the first few aircraft was the usual two 20 mm and four 0.303 in guns, but subsequent examples had two 20 mm and two 0.5 in guns, similar to the Mk IXE, fitted. This change called for a new designation, and thus we had the F Mk XIVE. The Griffon was very accommodating at all altitudes, and it was not found necessary to have low- or high-altitude variants.

Another change in the hitherto standard arrangement of fuel and oil tanks was the removal of the oil tank from under the engine, on account of the large crankcase of the Griffon, and its repositioning behind the fireproof bulkhead in front of the top main fuel tank in a similar manner to the Mk XII. This reduced the capacity of the main fuel tanks by some 10-11 gal, but it also kept the oil tank away from the engine, and allowed all the installation forward of the bulkhead to be produced as an interchangeable powerplant. This smaller top main fuel tank was not self-sealing.

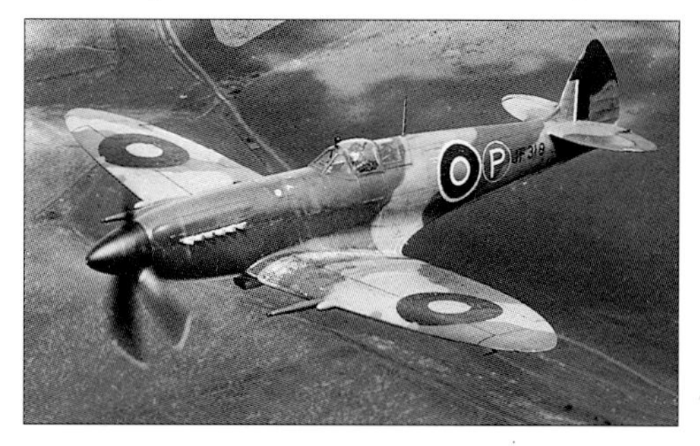

Spitfire F XIVC

The fuel in the two wing tanks was transferred to the top main tanks as on the VII and VIII, but via a new five-way selector cock instead of the plunger-type valve used in the earlier marks. The new cock was mounted on the left of the pilot and had positions for the transfer of either port or starboard wing tank, and for the normal venting under the control of the aneroid valve for pressurisation. Another innovation, introduced on this and subsequent marks, was the low level warning light which indicated to the pilot that there was sufficient fuel left for 30 minutes' flying.

The increased engine capacity called for larger radiators than hitherto, and the change in layout resulted in the oil cooler being behind the main radiator under the port wing, and the main radiator being behind the intercooler under the starboard wing. At the same time, the radiators were made deeper than on previous aircraft.

Up to this time, when a Spitfire or Seafire was being given an engine run on the ground, it had been sufficient to have chocks under the mainwheels, and two or three men applying their weight to the tailplane. With the Mk XIV, however, the increased weight and power of the Griffon 65 necessitated more positive lashing-down gear. Accordingly, larger chocks were made and joined together by a beam, and cables in Y-form were attached to the chocks and to a ring anchored in the ground under the tail. In addition, a large canvas band was placed round the fuselage at the base of the fin, and lashed to the same ring in the ground beneath. This complex procedure was very necessary, as during an engine run the up-load at the tail could become as much as 650 lbs. Indeed, on the first few aircraft, the load was sufficient to deform the lower leading edge of the fin where the band was restraining the tail. Reinforcement of the skin in this region soon cured the trouble.

With the Mk XIV, some changes were made in the armour protection. The ammunition boxes now had only top and bottom protection of heavy gauge light-alloy, and nothing in front. The plate behind the coolant header tank was removed, but a piece was fixed behind the top of the fireproof bulkhead to protect the oil tank. Another piece was introduced at the bottom of the windscreen, whilst the armour plate behind the pilot's seat was increased to two sheets varying from two to six inches apart. This was known as 'split' armour, and was designed to be most effective against 20 mm cannon ammunition.

The Mk XIV had a rate of climb that bettered 5000 ft per minute, and a top speed of 448 mph at an all-up weight of 8400 lbs. Its dimensions were 36 ft 10 in span and 32 ft 7 in long. The man-hours absorbed were 2600 in design and 1700 in jigs and tools.

In 1944, the Mk XIV were used to chase and destroy V1 flying bombs, but for this job it had special fuel, and could operate at 21 lb/in^2 boost.

Another use found for the Mk XIVE was photographic reconnaissance, and for this work an F24 oblique camera was installed in the rear fuselage. To give extra range, an extra fuel tank was fitted there also. It held 33 gal, had its own contents gauge, and was pressurised. The FR XIV, as it became known, had the clipped wings of the Mk XII, as it was to be used for low altitude, and also incorporated for the first time a 'rear view' cockpit hood.

Spitfire FR XIVE

This hood was of teardrop shape, and provided a much improved view for the pilot when he was returning home with precious pictures and wanted to see if he was being followed. The use of this hood necessitated the lowering of the top line of the aft fuselage, and meant extensive structural alterations to the frames and skin. The result gave the beloved Spitfire even sleeker lines, but actually it provided no increase in performance. At first the hood had to be moved fore-and-aft by hand like the old type, but later a chain and cable winding gear was introduced.

Seafire XV

By this time the Navy was looking for improvement in performance of Seafires, and was also becoming 'Griffon-conscious'. Accordingly, a new Seafire was produced to incorporate the latest ideas in power and efficiency. This resulted in a Seafire with a Griffon engine, folding wings and a small fuel tank in the leading edge of each wing. The engine was the Griffon VI of 1750 hp. It was installed in a similar manner to the Griffon IV on the Spitfire XII, although in this case there were no thermostats in the cooling system. Also, the supercharger was controlled manually instead of automatically.

Since mark numbers were now being allotted consecutively whether the aircraft was Spitfire or Seafire, this one became Seafire XV. Externally, it had the nose and tail of the Spitfire XII, and wings similar to those on the Seafire III, but including a 10 gal fuel tank in each leading edge. It also had a retractable tailwheel and a deck arrestor-hook.

On the first few Mk XVs, this hook was the A-frame unit of the Seafire III, but later aircraft had a newly-designed 'sting' hook anchored to the fuselage stern at the base of the rudder. The hook was spring-loaded in its housing and, when released, extended aft about 18 in. On release, the arm and housing of the hook were free to drop into the fully lowered position suitable for engaging the deck cables, and also to pivot laterally about 30°.

The lowering of the hook was assisted by an oleo-pneumatic damper which also prevented the hook from rebounding on hitting the deck. After a deck landing, the hook was stowed in the housing, the latter being locked up manually.

A feature of the early Seafire XV rudder was the trimming tab which extended aft of the trailing edge. When the sting hook was introduced, a portion of the base of the rudder was sacrificed, and in order to restore the effective area, the rudder was enlarged. The resulting outline of the rudder embraced the tab and was slightly taller than before. The hook housing was enclosed in a fairing which joined the lines of the rudder and fuselage, and the whole effect was quite visually pleasing. In addition, and when in flight with the hook locked up, this fairing provided some extra fin area.

Although there was no intercooler on the engine which necessitated an intercooler radiator, the external appearance was that of an aircraft fitted with just such a device. This was because the two familiar large radiator fairings were retained. In fact, the starboard fairing housed the coolant radiator, as always, and the port fairing housed an additional coolant radiator and also the oil cooler.

At this stage, the short, unused, 20 mm gun stub in the leading edge – previously apparent in the universal wing – disappeared. Another slight change regarding armament was the introduction of Mk V 20 mm guns in place of the Mk IIs. These guns had a shorter barrel and had to be cocked initially on the ground by hand, using a special cocking tool.

To prevent deck cables from fouling the tailwheel, a simple tubular guard was attached to the underside of the fuselage just forward of it.

The Seafire XV showed great improvement over the Mk III variants, having a top speed of over 390 mph, and a rate of climb of over 4000 ft per minute. The all-up weight was 8000 lbs, and the overall dimensions 36 ft 10 in span and 32 ft 3 in long (including the sting hook which extended several inches aft of the rudder trailing edge).

Spitfire XVI

This mark number was given to a new development of the outstanding LF IXE using a Merlin 266 engine - in other words, a Packard-built Merlin 66. There were slight differences in this engine installation compared with that of the British-built Merlins, one being that the supercharger gear change was operated electro-hydraulically instead of electro-pneumatically. The LF XVI, as it was called, also incorporated major modifications which had been introduced in the last Mk IXEs. The most important of these was the installation of two extra fuel tanks in the rear fuselage, their combined capacity being 66 gal, and a low-back fuselage. The later Mk IXs fitted with these two tanks had the normal hood, and therefore a deeper fuselage. The top tank of the two was larger than on the LF XVI, making the total capacity of the two tanks 74 gal.

Spitfire LF XVIE

The fuel supply from the rear tanks led straight to the engine, independent of the front main tanks, and was controlled by a separate cock on the port side of the cockpit. A feature of the lower of these two tanks was that the rudder and elevator cables passed straight through it, via tubes.

About this time, too, came the introduction of a 50 gal torpedo-shaped drop tank for current and future marks to supersede the 30 and 45 gal blister tanks. This new tank had clean lines, and was carried in the same fuselage fittings as the earlier tanks by means of four streamlined rods which had appropriate fittings at the top – two for the front hooks, one for the rear release fitting, and one for the fuel feed connection.

The canopy hood on this aircraft had no winding gear, as was introduced on the Mk XIV, but had to be moved fore-and-aft manually.

To keep the centre of gravity within limits when the two rear fuel tanks were installed, the air bottles and the oxygen bottles had to be moved from the rear of the fuselage forward into the wings, resulting in one of each per wing. Since this variant had the two 0.5 in and two 20 mm guns, the spaces in the wings hitherto occupied by the 0.303 in guns were utilised to house these bottles.

Another external recognition feature of the LF XVI, in addition to the teardrop hood, was the clipped wingtips which were standard for this type.

Quite a number of Spitfire LF XVIs were made, and they did useful work in low-altitude strafing towards the end of the war. Their performance was comparable to that of an LF IXE, but they had greater range. Their all-up weight was 7900 lbs.

Spitfires Mk 20 and 21

The end of 1943 saw the bringing together of all the improvements to date, and some others besides, into a Spitfire which was to be the last word in refinement and performance. Development of the Spitfire III using a Griffon engine had been planned long beforehand, and Mk IV was the title provisionally given to the type. Development on this variant, however, could not keep pace with that on types already well tried and, to avoid confusion, it was later called the Mk 20. Although only the prototype was built, it did, however, pave the way for the introduction of the Spitfire 21 which went into quantity production. At this stage, too, the mark numbers were changed from Roman to Arabic numerals.

Spitfire 21

The main difference between the Mk 21 and previous types was the completely redesigned wings. Stronger construction was necessary for the increased weight and performance aimed at, and slightly more wing area was required for high-altitude operation. Although the basic elliptical shape was retained, the wingtips were, at first, slightly more pointed than on previous wings, but on production aircraft the tips were rounded off again until the span was only one inch greater than that of the Mk XIV.

All the experience of the many different versions of the earlier wings was embodied, and provision made for one type of armament only – namely four 20 mm guns. These guns, two in each wing, were installed in a similar manner to earlier marks, and two small blisters were still required in the top surface of the wing to clear the belt feed mechanisms.

Another major change in the wing design was the positioning of the ailerons much further outboard than on earlier types. The attachment of the ailerons, too, was now by piano-type hinges instead of by two bearing-type hinges.

On the undersurface of the wings, the biggest change lay in the provision of fairing doors for the lower portion of the undercarriage wheel, hitherto unfaired when the undercarriage was retracted. Unlike the extra fairings on the mainwheel struts of the Mk III, which were hinged to the fixed fairings on the struts and operated by mechanical links, the doors on the Mk 21 were independently hinged to the outboard edges of the wheel bays, and were operated hydraulically.

To prevent the doors closing first and being fouled by the rising wheels, a sequence valve was installed in the hydraulic system to ensure that the strut was locked up before the door was closed.

The complication in designing the fairings, catches and locks to ensure that the fairings fitted closely and rigidly was repaid by the increase in performance gained by having a continuous smooth undersurface to the wings.

A further change relating to the wings was the housing of two small fuel tanks, with a combined capacity of 18 gal, in each leading edge.

The powerplant, five-bladed propeller and tail unit of the Mk 21 were similar to those of the Spitfire XIV, although the engine had a slightly different propeller reduction gear ratio, the engine being a Griffon 61 or 64 instead of the Griffon 65 of the Mk XIV. A few Mk 21s, however, were provided with a Griffon 85 engine, and fitted with a six-bladed contra-rotating propeller.

Another difference in the engine installation was the exchange of port and starboard radiator layouts. On the Mk 21, the oil cooler was behind the main radiator under the starboard wing, while the intercooler radiator was in front of the main radiator under the port wing. This was the fifth change in the disposition of the radiators. Another improvement necessary for the increased performance and all-up weight of this new type was the strengthening and lengthening of the mainwheel legs. The increased length gave the undercarriage a slightly wider track – 6 ft 8 in against the previous 5 ft 9 in.

The maximum speed of this variant was 450 mph.

Spitfire PR XIX

Spitfire PR XIX

Following the usual practice, as soon as Spitfires were available with powerful Griffon 61 series engines, the photographic reconnaissance units made their demands. Still more altitude and a higher top speed suited their needs admirably, but for the same reason as the fighter chaps they also wanted the advantage of a pressure-cabin. Having gained limited pressure-cabin experience with the Spitfire X, they were ready to go straight into operations with the best that could be provided.

Their new aircraft had the performance of a Spitfire XIV, a greater range than the PR XI, and the cockpit conditions of the PR X. The result was designated the PR XIX. Broadly, it was a Spitfire XIV with modified PR XI wings and other modifications necessitated by the pressure-cabin and the installation of cameras.

In general, the system for pressurisation of the cabin and hood were the same as for the Spitfire VII, except that for this aircraft the air intake and blower were on the port side of the engine rather than to starboard.

A spill valve was provided for bypassing the air when not required, and also a cock for controlling the supply of air to the hood seal. The hood and windscreen also had an air-drying system similar to that on the Spitfire VII, but in this case the windscreen was in one curved panel only, and not in three pieces with a bullet-proof insert.

In detail, the sealing of joints, and the design of control cable and pipe glands where they passed through the front and rear pressure bulkheads were an improvement on previous types.

The wings were a modified version of those used on the PR XI, with no armament, but with 66 gal leading-edge fuel tanks. The modification consisted of installing still extra fuel tanks between the spars, just outboard of the wheel bays, in the space occupied by the wing cameras on the PR XI. There was one 19 gal inter-spar tank in each wing. This gave a total fuel capacity of 252 gal, with the further option of a 90 gal or 170 gal drop tank – amazingly, the fuel capacity of the Spitfire I was a mere 85 gal!

To serve this extreme range, three oxygen bottles were installed.

The fuel in the inter-spar tanks was transferred to the top main fuselage tank in the usual way be air pressure from the vacuum pump, but in this instance it was not controlled by a transfer selector cock. Instead, the air pressure was delivered to the inter-spar tank continuously, but the entry of fuel into the top main tank was controlled by a float valve in that tank. This ensured that the fuel level in the main tank was maintained until the inter-spar tanks were empty. This system relieved the pilot of the necessity to watch the fuel gauge and judge when to switch over to the main tank supply. The air pressure in the transfer line was limited to $4^1/2$ lb/in^2 by the vacuum system relief valve.

The leading edge tanks had electric pumps and separate cocks, and fed direct to the engine. Each had its own contents gauge on the appropriate side of the cockpit. The drop tank also fed direct to the engine via its own cock.

The camera installations were somewhat similar to those in the Spitfire XI. The universal installation provided for either two fanned or a single F52 36 in vertical, two fanned F52 20 in vertical or two fanned F.24 14 in vertical and one F24 14 in or 8 in oblique. In addition, the wing camera installation as used on later PR XIs could be used in place of the inter-spar fuel tanks.

The fuselage cameras were heated by warm air collected in a scoop behind the starboard radiator and ducted to a sealing gland in the rear pressure bulkhead. Here, the duct divided into two rigid pipes going to the vertical camera lenses and windows, and one flexible pipe leading the air up to the oblique camera lens and window. The heat was prevented from dissipating too rapidly by a plywood bulkhead at the rear of the camera bay.

The wing camera bays also had warm air from behind the radiator conducted to them. The temperature of the camera bay was registered by a gauge on one side of the cockpit, while outside air temperature was registered on a gauge on the opposite side of the cockpit.

The all-up weight of the PR XIX was 7500 lb, and with its overall PR blue finish and no guns, the aircraft looked the last word in smooth, purposeful efficiency. Little wonder, then, that the PR XIX was the fastest Spitfire of them all, for it had a top speed of 460 mph – an increase of 100 mph over its eldest brother, the Mk I, whose own performance had been superlative in its day.

Spitfire XVIII

This variant was a further improvement along the lines of the Mks VII, VIII and XIV, and came into service a little later than the Mk 21.

In the main it was a Mk XIV with strengthened wings and undercarriage and extra fuel tankage. The extra fuel - 66 gal in the fuselage and $26^1/2$ gal in each wing – made it useful for reconnaissance, for which role it had alternative F24 or F52 camera installations. Even so, it had the same speed as the lighter Mk XIV.

Spitfire FR XVIIIE

Seafire XVII

This aircraft was developed from the Seafire XV, and was the first naval type to incorporate the teardrop hood. With this type of canopy also came a curved windscreen, in front of the bullet-proof portion. The larger rudder and faired sting arrestor-hook of the later Mk XVs were incorporated in this variant, as was provision for carrying wing bombs. The biggest change from the Mk XV, although not apparent externally, was the introduction of a 24V electrical system in place of the 12V system used hitherto in all Spitfires and Seafires.

Another innovation exclusive to the Navy was the provision in the Mk XVII for rocket-assisted take-off. This catered for the fitting, on each side of the fuselage at the root end of the wing, of a carrier to hold two rocket motors. The aircraft's electrical system was adapted to fire the rockets, and the carriers could be jettisoned after take-off, thus leaving the aircraft unencumbered by ancillary fittings. The rockets burned for approximately four seconds, and the take-off run was considerably reduced by their impetus.

The dimensions of the Mk XVII were the same as for the Mk XV, but the all-up weight was 500 lbs heavier at 8500 lbs. Even so, there was a slight increase in maximum speed over the Mk XV, and the Navy at last had an aircraft capable of 400 mph. At the other end of the speed range, the deck-landing characteristics were improved by the incorporation of long-stroke undercarriage shock-absorber struts, which provided a full travel of 8.0 in against the normal stroke of 4.9 in.

Seafire 45

Seafire 45

Still another Seafire came into being in 1945, this time a development of the Spitfire 21. Why it was numbered 45 is a clue to the many 'possibles' that were considered, using different combinations of engine, airframe and other special features. In spite of the large number of variants that went into production, there were still many 'pipedreams' which, for various reasons, got no further than the project stage. This particular variant, the Seafire 45, was simply a 'navalised' Spitfire 21, with deck arrestor-hood and naval radio.

The sting hook made the Seafire 45 the longest yet at 33 ft 4 in overall, but the span was unchanged from the Spitfire 21. The all-up weight, too, was the greatest yet at 9500 lbs, but the aircraft gave the Navy yet another 45 mph on the previous best top speed, as this type could reach almost 450 mph.

Seafire 45

This mark was an interim version pending the production of still more refined aircraft in the design stage, but it was a means of giving the Navy the best of what was available at the time, namely the Spitfire 21.

A few Seafire 45s were later given a Griffon 85 engine and a six-bladed contra-rotating propeller.

Seafire 46/47

These variants were the ultimate in the great range of development of the basic Spitfire aircraft. From a recognition point of view the most apparent differences between these and their forebears were the contra-rotating propellers, the teardrop hood and the increased fin and rudder area.

The former enabled still more power to be absorbed (Griffon 87 and 88 engine), and in particular obviated the inevitable torque effect of a single propeller when landing and taking off, especially on aircraft carriers. The teardrop gave better visibility and was combined with a smooth curved windscreen in place of the flat panel style of the earlier bullet-proof glass.

The increased fin and rudder area – now 23.08 ft^2 compared with the 18.345 ft^2 of the Mk 45 – was necessary to balance the propellers and extra-long spinner. Additional area was also provided in the tailplane and elevators, which now had 42.56 ft^2 against the earlier 33.84 ft^2.

The overall length was now 34 ft 6 in, although the span was not changed. Furthermore, the fairing on the underside of the engine on the FR 47 was improved to embrace the air intake filter and bring the opening of the duct right forward to just behind the propellers. This greatly improved the aerodynamic line along the underside of the aircraft.

Another concession to the Navy's requirements was the introduction in the FR 47 of a new wing-folding configuration. This time the hinge was outboard of the guns, the outer wing folding upwards while the wingtip remained fixed. This kept the height within 13 ft 10 in, although the folded span was 25 ft 5 in. At first, wing folding and spreading was carried out manually, and a strut was fitted to secure the wings when folded, but later hydraulic power folding and spreading was installed, and the strut was unnecessary.

With extra leading-edge fuel tanks, rear fuselage tanks, combat tanks and a 90 gal drop tank, it was possible for this version to carry 287 gals of fuel, giving it a range of about 1000 miles. Another 'best' achieved by this variant was a top speed of 452 mph.

For reconnaissance purposes some Mk 46s and all FR 47s had two electrically-heated cameras, one vertical and one oblique, in the rear of the fuselage. The vertical camera aperture in the bottom of the fuselage had a spring-loaded mudflap for protection during take-off. The flap was released in flight.

Seafire 47

The FR 47 was cleared for all forms of flying at 11,100 lbs all-up weight, but for take-off and gentle flying only it could weigh as much as 12,900 lbs. The distance between the forward and aft limits of the centre of gravity was only 6 in.

Spitfire 22 and 24

Spitfire 22

These two aircraft embodied the final stages in a long line of improvements, all of which entailed many hours of design and testing to achieve that little extra that would give the RAF and Navy the best possible aircraft of the day.

Retaining the basic features of the Mk 21, the Spitfires 22 and 24 were given the teardrop hood and extra tail-surface area, as for the Seafire 46. The aircraft's electrical system was also uprated to 24V instead of the earlier 12V.

The difference between the Mk 22 and 24 was the fuel capacity, the latter having rear-fuselage tanks and some refinement of rudder and elevator outline without a change in area.

Conclusion

Overall, some 22,750 Spitfires and Seafires were built. Their all-up weight increased from 5800 lbs to over 11,000 lbs, engine power increased from 1020 hp to 2050 hp, resulting in their speed increasing from 364 mph to 452 mph, and in total no fewer than 48 identifiable variants went into service.

INDEX